What Readers Are Saying About
iOS Recipes

If I had to pick just one person to learn from, to learn the best ways to do things in iOS, it would be Matt Drance. And the book doesn't disappoint. I made use of a couple recipes immediately, and I look forward to using more of them, especially Paul's fun graphics and animation recipes!

➤ **Brent Simmons**
  Developer, NetNewsWire

iOS Recipes is the book that commonly answers the "How did they do that?" question. It is an essential book for anyone who wants to sprinkle little bits of awesome in their app.

➤ **Justin Williams**
  Crew chief, Second Gear

This is a great book for both beginners and experienced developers. It's packed with useful up-to-date examples showing how to add professional-grade features to your projects, with great explanations and a focus on the code.

➤ **Michael Hay**
  Master developer, Black Pixel LLC

D1294293

I highly recommend this book. So many of these tips and tricks, aka recipes, get lost or become difficult to find. I would rather pull a book off the shelf (or iBooks) and look for that snippet of code I knew I saw in there rather than search the Internet in hope that the site I saw it on still has it. This book will definitely be in that collection.

➤ **Marcus S. Zarra**
   Owner, Zarra Studios LLC

If you use just one of these recipes in your app, that alone is worth the price of this book. I quickly lost count of the recipes that I found immediately useful. If you're getting paid to write iOS apps, or you just value your time, you'd be crazy not to have this book within arm's reach at all times.

➤ **Mike Clark**
   Founder, Clarkware

iOS Recipes

Tips and Tricks for Awesome iPhone and iPad Apps

Matt Drance

Paul Warren

The Pragmatic Bookshelf

Dallas, Texas • Raleigh, North Carolina

Many of the designations used by manufacturers and sellers to distinguish their products are claimed as trademarks. Where those designations appear in this book, and The Pragmatic Programmers, LLC was aware of a trademark claim, the designations have been printed in initial capital letters or in all capitals. The Pragmatic Starter Kit, The Pragmatic Programmer, Pragmatic Programming, Pragmatic Bookshelf, PragProg and the linking *g* device are trademarks of The Pragmatic Programmers, LLC.

Every precaution was taken in the preparation of this book. However, the publisher assumes no responsibility for errors or omissions, or for damages that may result from the use of information (including program listings) contained herein.

Our Pragmatic courses, workshops, and other products can help you and your team create better software and have more fun. For more information, as well as the latest Pragmatic titles, please visit us at *http://pragprog.com.*

The team that produced this book includes:

Jill Steinberg (editor)
Potomac Indexing, LLC (indexer)
Kim Wimpsett (copyeditor)
David J Kelly (typesetter)
Janet Furlow (producer)
Juliet Benda (rights)
Ellie Callahan (support)

Printed in the United States of America.
ISBN-13: 978-1-934356-74-6
Printed on acid-free paper.
Book version: P1.0—July 2011

Contents

Foreword vii

Introduction ix

Acknowledgments xiii

1. **UI Recipes** 1
   Recipe 1. Add a Basic Splash Screen Transition   2
   Recipe 2. Stylize Your Splash Screen Transition   10
   Recipe 3. Animate a Custom Notification View   16
   Recipe 4. Create Reusable Toggle Buttons   21
   Recipe 5. Form Rounded Views with Textured Colors   26
   Recipe 6. Put Together a Reusable Web View   29
   Recipe 7. Customize Sliders and Progress Views   33
   Recipe 8. Shape a Custom Gesture Recognizer   36
   Recipe 9. Create Self-contained Alert Views   40
   Recipe 10. Make a Label for Attributed Strings   46
   Recipe 11. Scroll an Infinite Wall of Album Art   51
   Recipe 12. Play Tracks from a Wall of Album Art   56
   Recipe 13. Have Fun with Autoscrolling Text Views   62
   Recipe 14. Create a Custom Number Control   66

2. **Table and Scroll View Recipes** 73
   Recipe 15. Simplify Table Cell Production   74
   Recipe 16. Use Smart Table Cells in a Nib   78
   Recipe 17. Locate Table Cell Subviews   83
   Recipe 18. Organize Complex Table Views   86
   Recipe 19. Produce Two-Tone Table Views   92
   Recipe 20. Add Border Shadows for Table Views   97
   Recipe 21. Place Static Content in a Zoomable Scroll View   104
   Recipe 22. Build a Carousel Paging Scroll View   109

3.	**Graphics Recipes**	**113**
	Recipe 23. Draw Gradient-Filled Bezier Paths	115
	Recipe 24. Create Dynamic Images with Multiple Animations	121
	Recipe 25. Make Composited and Transformed Views	124
	Recipe 26. Animate a Gradient Layer	127
	Recipe 27. Reshape Shadows	131
	Recipe 28. Display Animated Views	134
	Recipe 29. Construct a Simple Emitter	138
	Recipe 30. Curl the Page to a New View	143
4.	**Networking Recipes**	**149**
	Recipe 31. Tame the Network Activity Indicator	150
	Recipe 32. Simplify Web Service Connections	153
	Recipe 33. Format a Simple HTTP POST	157
	Recipe 34. Upload Files Over HTTP	162
5.	**Runtime Recipes**	**171**
	Recipe 35. Leverage Modern Objective-C Class Design	172
	Recipe 36. Produce Intelligent Debug Output	176
	Recipe 37. Design Smarter User Defaults Access	181
	Recipe 38. Scan and Traverse View Hierarchies	185
	Recipe 39. Initialize a Basic Data Model	192
	Recipe 40. Store Data in a Category	197

Foreword

iOS is an amazing platform to develop for. Its incredible touch screen and interaction paradigms have opened up entirely new categories of applications. We've already seen brilliant developers come up with software we could have barely imagined a few short years ago. The portability of the iPhone, iPod touch, and iPad means that we take them everywhere with us, and their reasonable battery life means that we use them constantly. Quite simply—and with apologies to the 2007 vintage MacBook Pro running Snow Leopard that I develop software and process my photos with—iOS is pointing the way to the future. It's obvious that computing has changed and won't be going back to the way it was in 2005.

Heady stuff, that. Who wouldn't want to develop software for these amazing devices?

On the other hand, the reality is that we've had only a few short years to start learning how to best develop software for the iOS and its touch-based frameworks. Sure, some of you have been creating software for Mac OS X and have a bit of a head start over the vast majority of you who have come to iOS development from other platforms. Make no mistake, however. No matter what your background, we all find ourselves in a new land when it comes to writing for iOS. Even though I wrote my first Cocoa app more than a decade ago and have written more than my share of books and articles on Mac OS X development, I've had more than a few head-scratching sessions as I've worked with iOS and dove through its documentation in Xcode. There's so much to figure out, including how to create perfect splash screens, how to make table and scroll views do our bidding most efficiently, how to access the many network services modern social applications use, and how to work with the iOS runtime instead of fighting against it.

Luckily, we don't have to sort all of these things out on our own. Matt and Paul—the authors of this book—have assembled a set of examples and incorporated the latest, most current iOS software development best practices in this book of recipes. The result gives you a great set of specific solutions to targeted problems that you can dip in and out of as the need arises.

It's better than that, however. Even though this book is a collection of discrete sections that can stand on their own quite well, reading straight through them all gives more than a few valuable insights into how Matt and Paul approach their craft. As I read through a beta draft of the book myself, it felt much the same as watching some of my favorite chefs making good food in their kitchen and learning from the way they approached the task at hand, even the simple tasks that I thought I already had mastered.

So, pull up a chair. Join two of my favorite iOS developers and learn a few things. Then, go out and make the kind software you could only dream about a few years ago.

James Duncan Davidson

April 2011

Introduction

Your goal as a programmer is to solve problems. Sometimes the problems are hard, sometimes they're easy, and sometimes they're even fun. Maybe they're not even "problems" in the colloquial sense of the word, but you are there to discover solutions.

Our goal as authors is to help you solve your problems better and more quickly than before—preferably in that order. We decided to write a recipe-style book that focuses on a specific set of tasks and problems that we attack explicitly, rather than discuss programming issues at a high level.

That's not to say we're not about educating in this book. The blessing of a recipe book is that it gives you trustworthy solutions to problems that you don't feel like discovering on your own. The curse of a recipe book is that you might be tempted to copy and paste the solutions into your project without taking the time to understand them. It's always great to save time by writing less code, but it's just as great to think and learn about how you saved that time and how you can save more of it moving forward.

If you are familiar with the iOS SDK and are looking to improve the quality and efficiency of your apps, then this book is for you. We don't teach you how to write apps here, but we hope that this book helps you make them better. If you're more of an advanced developer, you may find that you save yourself time and trouble by adopting some of the more sophisticated techniques laid out in the pages that follow.

We wrote many of these recipes with maximum reusability in mind. We weren't after demonstrating a technique or a snippet of code that simply gets the job done. Instead, we set out to build solutions that are ready for you to integrate into whatever iPad and iPhone projects you're working on. Some might find their way into your projects with zero changes, but you should feel free to use this recipe book as you would a traditional cookbook. When cooking food from a recipe, you might add or remove ingredients based on what you like, or need, in a meal. When it comes to your own apps and projects, this book is no different: you are invited to extend and edit the projects that accompany these recipes to fit your specific needs.

The recipes in this book help you get from start to finish, but we hope they also encourage you to think about when and why to choose a certain path. There are often multiple options, especially in an environment like Cocoa. With multiple options, of course, come multiple opinions. In the interest of consistency, we made some decisions early on about certain patterns and approaches to use in this book. Some of these techniques may be familiar to you, some may be employed in a way you hadn't considered, and some may be brand new to you. Regardless, we'd like to explain some of our decisions up front so that there are no surprises.

Formatting and Syntax

We had to format a few code snippets in this book to fit the page. A verbose language like Objective-C doesn't always play nicely with character limits, so some of the code may sometimes look unusual. You may encounter terse method or variable names, a seemingly excessive number of temporary variables, and odd carriage returns. We tried to preserve the "spirit" of Cocoa convention as much as possible, but in a few places the printed page won. Don't be alarmed if the coding style suddenly changes from time to time.

Categories

A fair number of recipes make use of categories on standard Apple classes to accomplish tasks. Categories are an incredibly powerful feature of the Objective-C programming language, and they tend to alienate new Cocoa programmers. Categories can also quickly pollute namespaces and create (or mask) unexpected behavior in complex class hierarchies. They aren't to be feared, but they are to be respected. When considering a category, do the following:

- Ask yourself whether a subclass or a new class would be more appropriate. As *The Objective-C Programming Language* from Apple states, "A category is not a substitute for a subclass."

- *Always* prefix category methods when extending a class you don't control (for example, UIApplication) to avoid symbol collisions with future APIs. All new category methods in this book use a prp_ prefix.

- *Never* override defined methods such as -drawRect: in a category. You'll break the inheritance tree by masking the source class implementation.

Synthesized Instance Variables

You'll find few, if any, instance variable (*ivar*) declarations in the header files and examples that accompany this book. We've chosen to exclusively use Objective-C 2.0 properties, with the modern runtime's ivar synthesis feature, for declaring class storage. The result is less typing and less reading so we can concentrate on the recipe itself. We explain this further in Recipe 35, *Leverage Modern Objective-C Class Design*, on page 172.

Private Class Extensions

Private class extensions are another relatively new feature of Objective-C, and we use them frequently in this book. Private extensions can increase readability by minimizing header noise, and they also paint a much clearer picture for adopters or maintainers of your code. In Recipe 35, *Leverage Modern Objective-C Class Design*, on page 172 we introduce both private class extensions and synthesized instance variables for anyone unfamiliar with either technique.

Cleanup in -dealloc

In addition to releasing all relevant instance variables in the -dealloc, our examples set them to nil. This practice is one of the most hotly debated topics among Cocoa programmers, and both sides of the argument hold weight. This book is not meant to participate in the debate at all: we set them to nil, but that doesn't mean *you* have to do so. If you don't like nil-in--dealloc, feel free to leave it out of your own code.

Blocks vs. Delegation

Blocks are a new feature added to C and Objective-C in Mac OS X Snow Leopard and iOS 4.0. Because of the relative youth of this feature, the debate on when to use blocks or delegates remains heated. In the book we use both at what we felt were appropriate times. You're more than welcome to add blocks to a recipe that uses delegates, or vice versa. Our goal is ultimately to help you find the simplest and most natural solutions you can.

Above all, this book is about reducing complexity and repetition in your code. Rather than go for the quick fix to a problem, we opted for solutions that will be readily available for the long haul. We hope that the ideas in these pages assist you in your journey as an iOS developer.

Online Resources

This book has its own web page, http://pragprog.com/titles/cdirec, where you can find more information about the book and interact in the following ways:

- Access the full source code for all the sample programs used in this book

- Participate in a discussion forum with other readers, iOS developers, and the authors

- Help improve the book by reporting errata, including content suggestions and typos

Note: If you're reading the ebook, you can also click the gray-green rectangle before the code listings to download that source file directly.

Acknowledgments

We had an all-star cast of reviewers for this book, and they all deserve recognition for giving us even a tiny bit of their incredibly valuable time. Colin Barrett, Mike Clark, Michael Hay, Daniel Steinberg, Justin Williams, and Marcus Zarra were generous, forthcoming, and motivated in helping us make this book as good as it could be. The feedback we received over email, Twitter, iChat, lunches, and the forums at PragProg.com was just as important in getting us to this point. Thank you all for your contributions to this book.

Matt Drance

You don't write a book like this unless you love the subject. This book's subject was born from the tireless effort of hundreds of gifted and passionate people in Cupertino over the better part of the past decade. I must thank my many friends and former colleagues at Apple for creating this wonderful platform: engineers, product managers, evangelists, technical writers, support staff...everyone. You can't produce something like iOS without all hands on deck at all times.

Although Apple made this book possible, Dave, Andy, Susannah, and the rest of the PragProg staff made it reality. Our editor, Jill Steinberg, has been a truly fearless and patient leader while I ran off to day jobs and other distractions. Writing a book has always been a personal goal of mine, and I am pleased to have done it so early in life. Thank you all for giving me the chance.

The biggest thanks of all, however, go to my friends and family for supporting me through this journey. My wonderful wife and son are the real reason I do anything. This indie developer gig ain't bad, but it doesn't come close to being a husband or a dad.

Paul Warren

I'd like to add my appreciation for the work of the wonderful people at Apple for building this amazing platform that is our daily playground. Also to Jill and the team at PragProg.com for providing a delightfully nurturing experience. And to our extraordinary community of developers who share and encourage in equal measure.

The phrase "What do you think of this?" will no doubt haunt the dreams of my beautiful wife and daughters, who showed remarkable patience with a fledgling author in the house. For that, and for filling my life with the sounds and love of an amazingly supportive family, I will be continually amazed and grateful.

CHAPTER 1

UI Recipes

We could easily write an entire book on UI recipes. After all, the iOS SDK has a seemingly endless library of classes and patterns that are definitely worth discussing. Ultimately we decided to focus on presenting good solutions to some simple patterns and problems—the kinds of things you find yourself doing over and over again without quite remembering how you did it the last time.

In this section we introduce recipes on view transitions, web content, touch handling, and even custom controls. These recipes are ready for you to use and might just inspire you to think about making your own code ready for reuse in your next inevitable project.

Recipe 1

Add a Basic Splash Screen Transition

Problem

A harsh transition from the default image to the live UI on startup creates a bad first impression for your users. You want the transition from your app's startup image to your initial UI to be as smooth as possible, but you're not sure how to go about this in the cleanest way.

Solution

The visual experience of an iOS app launching goes something like this:

1. User taps an app icon.

2. App's default image scales onto the screen.

3. App's initial UI is loaded into memory.

4. UI appears on-screen and replaces the default image.

If your default image is a branded banner or some other stylized picture, your users might see a harsh transition to the live UI. You want to introduce a smooth transition from the splash screen to your running application. There are plenty of ways to do this, but let's start with a very simple approach that should be usable from just about anywhere. We'll start by tackling an iPhone app in portrait orientation and then move on to an iPad variant that supports all orientations. You can see the initial screens in Figure 1, *Splash screen vs. initial UI*, on page 3.

The simplest possible "splash screen transition" is a fade between the default image and the UI. It's cheap and easy and can make a world of difference for the user experience. Think about it: this is the very first thing your users see. There's no reason for this introduction to be anything but smooth.

To fade the default image offscreen, we need to first show a view that displays the same image and then fade that view out. This is pretty easy to do: we're going to build a simple view controller that's usable from just about any project. This view controller takes a custom splash image and defines a -hide method that executes the fade.

Figure 1—Splash screen vs. initial UI

BasicSplashScreen/PRPSplashScreen.h
```
@interface PRPSplashScreen : UIViewController {}

@property (nonatomic, retain) UIImage *splashImage;
@property (nonatomic, assign) BOOL showsStatusBarOnDismissal;
@property (nonatomic, assign) IBOutlet id<PRPSplashScreenDelegate> delegate;

- (void)hide;

@end
```

The interface also has a delegate property, declared as an id <PRPSplashScreen-Delegate>. That PRPSplashScreenDelegate protocol is defined in a separate header for communicating the splash screen's status to an interested party: when the screen appears, when the transition begins, and when it ends.

You've surely acted as a delegate in plenty of places, but you may not have defined one before. Take a look at the protocol declaration and note the @optional keyword, which means the delegate does not have to implement all of the declared methods. An object that wants to know the splash screen's state can now declare itself as conforming to PRPSplashScreenDelegate, implement one or more of the delegate methods, and assign itself to the splash screen's delegate property.

BasicSplashScreen/PRPSplashScreenDelegate.h

```
@protocol PRPSplashScreenDelegate <NSObject>

@optional
- (void)splashScreenDidAppear:(PRPSplashScreen *)splashScreen;
- (void)splashScreenWillDisappear:(PRPSplashScreen *)splashScreen;
- (void)splashScreenDidDisappear:(PRPSplashScreen *)splashScreen;

@end
```

PRPSplashScreen builds its view in -loadView so you don't have to drag a XIB file around every time you need it. This makes it a little easier to drop into projects. The view property is set to a single image view that fills the screen and centers its image.

BasicSplashScreen/PRPSplashScreen.m

```
- (void)loadView {
    UIImageView *iv = [[UIImageView alloc] initWithImage:self.splashImage];
    iv.autoresizingMask = UIViewAutoresizingFlexibleWidth |
        UIViewAutoresizingFlexibleHeight;
    iv.contentMode = UIViewContentModeCenter;
    self.view = iv;
    [iv release];
}
```

Now let's take a look at the splashImage property. It's writable, so if you want to set a custom transition image, you can. But you may just want to use Default.png as the splash image, since the whole point of this recipe is to create a smooth transition. So, we write a lazy initializer that loads Default.png by default. If you're transitioning from your default image, you don't need to touch this property. We use +[UIImage imageNamed:] to ensure an image with the appropriate scale (for example, Default@2x.png for Retina displays) is used.

BasicSplashScreen/PRPSplashScreen.m

```
- (UIImage *)splashImage {
    if (splashImage == nil) {
        self.splashImage = [UIImage imageNamed:@"Default.png"];
    }
    return splashImage;
}
```

Setting up the splash screen is easy: just present it as a modal view controller off your application's root view controller. We'll do this at launch time, before showing the main window but after adding the root view. This timing is important: the root view controller won't properly present a modal view controller if its own view isn't in place. In the BasicSplashScreen project accompanying this recipe, we also specify a dissolve-style (fade) transition in the code. Because the splash screen uses the launch image by default, we don't need to specify one ourselves.

```
BasicSplashScreen/iPhone/AppDelegate_iPhone.m
- (BOOL)application:(UIApplication *)application
        didFinishLaunchingWithOptions:(NSDictionary *)launchOptions {
    [self.window addSubview:self.navController.view];
    self.splashScreen.showsStatusBarOnDismissal = YES;
    self.splashScreen.modalTransitionStyle =
                                UIModalTransitionStyleCrossDissolve;
    [self.navController presentModalViewController:splashScreen
                                    animated:NO];
    [self.window makeKeyAndVisible];
    return YES;
}
```

If you open MainWindow_iPhone.xib, you'll see a PRPSplashScreen object defined in the XIB. (See Figure 2, *Connecting the splash screen in Interface Builder*, on page 6.) This object is connected to the app delegate's splashScreen property in Interface Builder. The previous code references this property in order to kick off the splash transition.

Once the window becomes visible, the splash screen view controller receives the standard UIViewController messages, including -viewDidAppear :. This is the cue to begin the transition, and it's very simple. We first alert the delegate that the splash view appeared, in case the delegate needs to prepare for the transition. It's important to first check whether the delegate has implemented the appropriate methods, because we declared them as optional in our delegate protocol. After messaging the delegate, we send -hide to perform the splash transition. Note that we use performSelector:withObject:afterDelay: here, which gives the UIKit run loop an opportunity to finalize the viewDidAppear machinery. Dismissing a view controller from within its own viewWillAppear: or viewDidAppear: method can confuse the system—each action needs to be separate and discrete.

```
BasicSplashScreen/PRPsplashScreen.m
- (void)viewDidAppear:(BOOL)animated {
    [super viewDidAppear:animated];
    SEL didAppearSelector = @selector(splashScreenDidAppear:);
    if ([self.delegate respondsToSelector:didAppearSelector]) {
        [self.delegate splashScreenDidAppear:self];
    }
    [self performSelector:@selector(hide) withObject:nil afterDelay:0];
}
```

The -hide method uses the standard -dismissModalViewControllerAnimated: method to perform the transition, after checking whether it should show the status

The splash screen is initialized from the respective MainWindow XIB file and connected to the app delegate's splashScreen property. The app delegate is also connected as the splash screen's delegate.

Figure 2—Connecting the splash screen in Interface Builder

bar while fading out. This is added in case you don't want the status bar shown at launch but do want it on the UI. To enable this effect, set UIStatusBarHidden to YES in your app's Info.plist file, and set the splash screen's showsStatusBarOnDismissal property to YES. The splash screen manages the status bar's reactivation so you don't need to do it yourself in one of the delegate methods (see Figure 3, *Hiding the status bar on launch*, on page 7).

BasicSplashScreen/PRPSplashScreen.m
```
- (void)hide {
    if (self.showsStatusBarOnDismissal) {
        UIApplication *app = [UIApplication sharedApplication];
        [app setStatusBarHidden:NO withAnimation:UIStatusBarAnimationFade];
    }
    [self dismissModalViewControllerAnimated:YES];
}
```

The splash screen also keeps the delegate informed of the transition's progress by relaying the standard -viewWillDisappear: and -viewDidDisappear: view controller methods. The app delegate uses the corresponding -splashScreenDidDisappear: delegate method to remove the splash screen once it's not needed.

BasicSplashScreen/iPhone/AppDelegate_iPhone.m
```
- (void)splashScreenDidDisappear:(PRPSplashScreen *)splashScreen {
    self.splashScreen = nil;
}
```

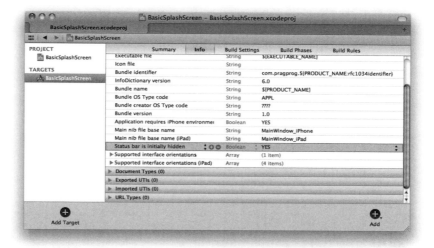

Set the UIStatusBarHidden key to YES to hide the status bar on launch. If you want to show it in your main UI, set the splash screen's showsStatusBarOnDismissal property to YES.

Figure 3—Hiding the status bar on launch

Run the BasicSplashScreen project, targeting iPhone, to see the transition from splash screen to UI. The delegate connection is set in MainWindow_iPhone.xib and MainWindow_iPad.xib, which is why you don't see the delegate property accessed anywhere in the code. The PRPWebViewController class, which we use to display the book details, is explained in detail in Recipe 6, *Put Together a Reusable Web View*, on page 29.

The solution so far performs a portrait-only transition, which is usually fine for most iPhone apps. iPad apps, on the other hand, are often expected to work in both portrait and landscape modes. Because UIViewController provides autorotation behavior for free and PRPSplashScreen inherits from UIViewController, supporting multiple orientations is fairly simple. We'll start by creating an iPad-specific subclass of PRPSplashScreen that adds support for all orientations.

BasicSplashScreen/iPad/PRPSplashScreen_iPad.m
```
- (BOOL)shouldAutorotateToInterfaceOrientation:
        (UIInterfaceOrientation)toInterfaceOrientation {
    return YES;
}
```

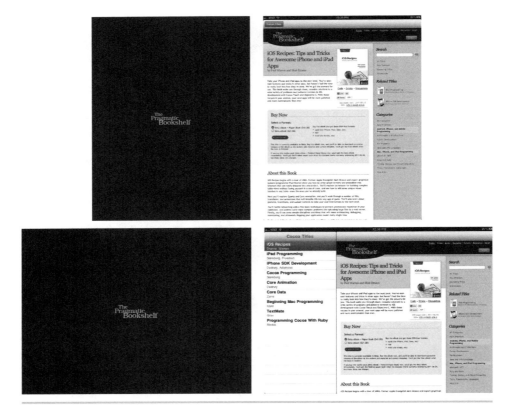

Figure 4—Multiple orientations on iPad

This is the only addition this subclass makes; all the other behavior from PRPSplashScreen is unchanged.

The only thing left is to supply a new splash image. When supporting multiple launch orientations, you supply both portrait and landscape variants of your default image, and UIKit chooses the right one for you. However, your code has no way of knowing which image was used and therefore can't choose the right one for your splash screen view. We could detect the device orientation from UIDevice or the status bar orientation from UIApplication, but there's an even easier way. Since our goal is to keep the logo centered, we simply make a new splash image resized to 1024x1024 pixels. This size meets the maximum screen size in both orientations and will remain centered while also filling the screen, no matter how the device is rotated. It will even stay centered if a live rotation occurs before the transition. We include this image in the app and set it as the splash screen's designated splash image, using the splashImage property defined by PRPSplashScreen.

BasicSplashScreen/iPad/AppDelegate_iPad.m

```
- (BOOL)application:(UIApplication *)application
        didFinishLaunchingWithOptions:(NSDictionary *)launchOptions {
    [self.window addSubview:self.splitViewController.view];

    UIImage *splash = [UIImage imageNamed:@"splash_background_ipad.png"];
    self.splashScreen.splashImage = splash;

    self.splashScreen.showsStatusBarOnDismissal = YES;
    self.splashScreen.modalTransitionStyle =
                                    UIModalTransitionStyleCrossDissolve;
    [self.splitViewController presentModalViewController:splashScreen
                                        animated:NO];

    [self.window makeKeyAndVisible];

    return YES;
}
```

The rest of the initialization code is identical to the iPhone variant. Run Ba-sicSplashScreen for the iPad, and observe the seamless transition in both portrait and landscape modes, as you can see in Figure 4, *Multiple orientations on iPad*, on page 8. We've now produced an easily reusable basic transition from our stylized default image to our app's initial UI, on both the iPhone and iPad.

Recipe 2

Stylize Your Splash Screen Transition

Problem

It's one thing to create a clean splash screen transition, but sometimes it would be nice to go beyond a basic fade and give the transition more finesse.

Solution

In Recipe 1, *Add a Basic Splash Screen Transition*, on page 2 we discussed the importance of a splash screen transition and how it makes a world of difference in the user experience. In that first recipe we were primarily concerned with establishing a clean structure to implement the transition, but the fade transition, though elegant, was the simplest we could use. Although we still want this introduction to be smooth, we can produce some attractive alternatives by exploring some masking techniques combined with Core Animation.

As in the previous example, in order to transition the default image offscreen, first we need to present a view that displays the default image, and then we need to gradually remove that view, revealing the primary interface view that lies behind (see Figure 5, *The CircleFromCenter transition in action*, on page 11).

Though we explore several examples in this recipe, they share the same basic masking technique. We use a mask to exclude part of the image and then animate the mask's *scale* until the image has been effectively removed.

Every view we create is backed by a layer, a graphic element that is directly drawn by the graphics processor. The layer behaves as an image store, allowing the view to be manipulated (moved, scaled, rotated) without the need to be redrawn. We can modify the layer properties directly, which gives us further options for modifying the presentation of the view. One of these properties is the mask property, which allows us to specify a second layer whose alpha channel will be used to *mask* the image of the layer. The alpha channel of an image specifies those areas that have varying levels of transparency, from 0 (Transparent) to 1 (Opaque). When a layer mask is added to the view, any sections of the mask image that are opaque display the

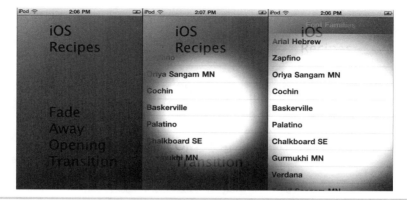

Figure 5—The CircleFromCenter transition in action

original image, but any areas that are transparent or partially transparent show through some, or all, of the view that lies below (see Figure 6, *The mask used for CircleFromCenter transition*, on page 12).

We use predefined images to create the contents for the mask layer, each with different areas of opacity to help create the effect we are seeking. We then animate an increase in scale of the mask layer, effectively expanding its size, to completely cover the view and render it transparent.

The anchorPoint of the mask layer is extremely important. When we change the scale of the layer using a transform, the stretch effect will be centered around the anchorPoint, so our anchorPoint needs to match the center of the transparent portion of our mask. This gives the effect that the clear portion of the mask is expanding, resulting in the gradual reveal of the view below. (See Figure 7, *The mask used for ClearFromCenter transition*, on page 12.)

In the viewDidLoad method, we add the copy of the Default.png image; this helps create the impression that the original splash screen has not been removed. To avoid using an UIImageView, we directly fill the contents of the view's layer, while also setting the scale factor to match the device. To avoid the replacement image being offset by the status bar, set the contentMode to UIViewContentModeBottom; this keeps the image anchored to the bottom of the screen.

SplashScreenReveal/PRPSplashScreenViewController.m
```
- (void)viewDidLoad {
    self.view.layer.contentsScale = [[UIScreen mainScreen] scale];
    self.view.layer.contents = (id)self.splashImage.CGImage;
    self.view.contentMode = UIViewContentModeBottom;
    if (self.transition == 0) self.transition = ClearFromRight;
}
```

Figure 6—The mask used for CircleFromCenter transition

Figure 7—The mask used for ClearFromCenter transition

In the viewDidAppear: method we use a Switch statement to match the Enum to the transition type. We need adjust only two elements for each one: the mask image and the associated anchorPoint. The performSelector:withObject:afterDelay: method is useful here because it allows us to create a delay before we activate the animate method and start the transition.

SplashScreenReveal/PRPSplashScreenViewController.m

```objc
- (void)viewDidAppear:(BOOL)animated {
    if ([self.delegate respondsToSelector:@selector(splashScreenDidAppear:)]) {
        [self.delegate splashScreenDidAppear:self];
    }
    switch (self.transition) {
        case CircleFromCenter:
            self.maskImageName = @"mask";
            self.anchor = CGPointMake(0.5, 0.5);
            break;
        case ClearFromCenter:
            self.maskImageName = @"wideMask";
            self.anchor = CGPointMake(0.5, 0.5);
            break;
        case ClearFromLeft:
            self.maskImageName = @"leftStripMask";
            self.anchor = CGPointMake(0.0, 0.5);
            break;
        case ClearFromRight:
            self.maskImageName = @"RightStripMask";
            self.anchor = CGPointMake(1.0, 0.5);
            break;
        case ClearFromTop:
            self.maskImageName = @"TopStripMask";
            self.anchor = CGPointMake(0.5, 0.0);
            break;
        case ClearFromBottom:
            self.maskImageName = @"BottomStripMask";
            self.anchor = CGPointMake(0.5, 1.0);
            break;
        default:
            return;
    }
    [self performSelector:@selector(animate)
                               withObject:nil
                               afterDelay:self.delay];
}
```

The only active part of our transition is the animation of the mask layer. We need to increase the scale, effectively enlarging the layer, until we have stretched the transparent portion of the mask to cover the whole view. The toValue we use here contains a bit of fudge factor but is calculated to make the mask large enough to complete the reveal. If we were to significantly modify the mask image, we might need to adjust this calculation.

SplashScreenReveal/PRPSplashScreenViewController.m

```
- (void)animate {
    if ([self.delegate respondsToSelector:@selector(splashScreenWillDisappear:)]) {
        [self.delegate splashScreenWillDisappear:self];
    }

    [self setMaskLayerwithanchor];

    CABasicAnimation *anim = [CABasicAnimation
                              animationWithKeyPath:@"transform.scale"];
    anim.duration = DURATION;
    anim.toValue = [NSNumber numberWithInt:self.view.bounds.size.height/8];
    anim.fillMode = kCAFillModeBoth;
    anim.removedOnCompletion = NO;
    anim.delegate = self;
    [self.view.layer.mask addAnimation:anim forKey:@"scale" ];

}
```

In the setMaskLayerwithanchor method, we need to create the mask layer for our effect, set its contents to the appropriate mask image, and set the correct anchor point to ensure that the seed point of opacity on the mask coincides with the anchor point.

SplashScreenReveal/PRPSplashScreenViewController.m

```
- (void)setMaskLayerwithanchor {

    CALayer *maskLayer = [CALayer layer];
    maskLayer.anchorPoint = self.anchor;
    maskLayer.frame = self.view.superview.frame;
    maskLayer.contents = (id)self.maskImage.CGImage;
    self.view.layer.mask = maskLayer;
}
```

Based on the selected Enum, we need to fetch and set the correct mask image for the required transition.

SplashScreenReveal/PRPSplashScreenViewController.m

```
- (UIImage *)maskImage {
    if (maskImage != nil) [maskImage release];
    NSString *defaultPath = [[NSBundle mainBundle]
                             pathForResource:self.maskImageName
                             ofType:@"png"];
    maskImage = [[UIImage alloc]
                 initWithContentsOfFile:defaultPath];
    return maskImage;
}
```

The animationDidStop delegate is called once the animation has finished stretching the mask layer. The transitioned view now appears to have been removed, so all we need to do here is remove it from the SuperView and notify the delegate that the transition has completed.

```
SplashScreenReveal/PRPSplashScreenViewController.m
- (void)animationDidStop:(CAAnimation *)theAnimation finished:(BOOL)flag {

    self.view.layer.mask = nil;
    [self.view removeFromSuperview];
    if ([self.delegate respondsToSelector:@selector(splashScreenDidDisappear:)]) {
        [self.delegate splashScreenDidDisappear:self];
    }
}
```

The gradual reveal transition adds a little more polish to the opening of your app and is easily extended to provide more options. The shape of the transparent area of the mask is maintained as it scales, so alternate shapes could yield interesting effects—star shapes, for example. You could even use more complex shapes, such as faces, but it may then be necessary to add an additional fade animation to remove any residual visual elements.

Recipe 3

Animate a Custom Notification View

Problem

Sometimes you need to signal that something has changed in your app—perhaps the completion of a background task. The notification mechanisms Apple provides—UIAlertView, for example—are generally modal, which is not always ideal because the notification pulls the user's attention away from the main app and requires a touch to dismiss. How can you create a nonmodal mechanism that attracts attention but can be easily ignored?

Solution

You need a solution that is reasonably generic and doesn't depend too much on the layout of your app. There are several techniques to choose from, but for this recipe we'll use a UIView that slides onto the screen and can be dismissed with a touch *or* can remove itself after a set amount of time. Using a slide animation should get the user's attention but still be easy to ignore, assuming we don't cover too much of the screen with the animation.

We create a UIView subclass, SlideInView, which exposes two methods: showWithTimer:inView:from:, which controls its appearance and timing, and viewWithImage:, which is a class method that instantiates the view from a UIImage. We can also create the view in Interface Builder, which allows for more dynamic notifications that can include labels and images. By using labels, we can reuse slideInViews by simply modifying the text in the label (see Figure 8, *SlideInView sample app*, on page 17).

SlideInView/SlideInView.m
```
+ (id)viewWithImage:(UIImage *)SlideInImage {

    SlideInView *SlideIn = [[[SlideInView alloc] init] autorelease];
    SlideIn.imageSize = SlideInImage.size;
    SlideIn.layer.bounds = CGRectMake(0, 0, SlideIn.imageSize.width,
                                      SlideIn.imageSize.height);
    SlideIn.layer.anchorPoint = CGPointMake(0, 0);
    SlideIn.layer.position = CGPointMake(-SlideIn.imageSize.width, 0);
    SlideIn.layer.contents = (id)SlideInImage.CGImage;
    return SlideIn;
}
```

Figure 8—SlideInView sample app

The class method viewWithImage: instantiates the view and sets the contents property of the underlying layer to point to the UIImage. The view position is set to be offscreen, but it will need to be adjusted again depending on the direction and position of the animation.

SlideInView/SlideInView.m
```
- (void)awakeFromNib {

    self.imageSize = self.frame.size;
    self.layer.bounds = CGRectMake(0, 0, self.imageSize.width,
                                         self.imageSize.height);
    self.layer.anchorPoint = CGPointMake(0, 0);
    self.layer.position = CGPointMake(-self.imageSize.width, 0);
}
```

The awakeFromNib() method is called after the instance of SlideInView has already been unpacked, so we just need to ensure that the view is positioned off the screen.

SlideInView/SlideInView.m

```
switch (side) {                      //  align view and set adjustment value
  case SlideInViewTop:
    self.adjustY = self.imageSize.height;
    fromPos = CGPointMake(view.frame.size.width/2-self.imageSize.width/2,
                          -self.imageSize.height);
    break;
  case SlideInViewBot:
    self.adjustY = -self.imageSize.height;
    fromPos = CGPointMake(view.frame.size.width/2-self.imageSize.width/2,
                          view.bounds.size.height);
    break;
  case SlideInViewLeft:
    self.adjustX = self.imageSize.width;
    fromPos = CGPointMake(-self.imageSize.width,
                          view.frame.size.height/2-self.imageSize.height/2);
                break;
  case SlideInViewRight:
    self.adjustX = -self.imageSize.width;
    fromPos = CGPointMake(view.bounds.size.width,
                          view.frame.size.height/2-self.imageSize.height/2);
  break;
  default:
    return;
  }
```

The showWithTimer:inView:from:bounce: method takes three parameters: the destination view, the enum representing the side to slide from, and the option to
add an additional bounce element to the slide animation. Based on the side
enum, we set the adjustX or adjustY value that is used to calculate the end point
of the animation, and we set the fromPos value for the view to start offscreen
on the selected side.

SlideInView/SlideInView.m

```
CGPoint toPos = fromPos;
CGPoint bouncePos = fromPos;
bouncePos.x += (adjustX*1.2);
bouncePos.y += (adjustY*1.2);
toPos.x += adjustX;
toPos.y += adjustY;

CAKeyframeAnimation *keyFrame = [CAKeyframeAnimation
                                  animationWithKeyPath:@"position"];
keyFrame.values  = [NSArray arrayWithObjects:
                    [NSValue valueWithCGPoint:fromPos],
                    [NSValue valueWithCGPoint:bouncePos],
                    [NSValue valueWithCGPoint:toPos],
                    [NSValue valueWithCGPoint:bouncePos],
                    [NSValue valueWithCGPoint:toPos],
                    nil];
```

```
keyFrame.keyTimes = [NSArray arrayWithObjects:
                      [NSNumber numberWithFloat:0],
                      [NSNumber numberWithFloat:.18],
                      [NSNumber numberWithFloat:.5],
                      [NSNumber numberWithFloat:.75],
                      [NSNumber numberWithFloat:1],
                      nil];
```

The bounce option triggers the use of keyframe animation, adding the extra values and keyTimes necessary to give the impression of a small bounce in the appropriate direction. Keyframe animation is a powerful and flexible technique for creating nonstandard animation curves. The keyTimes are unit values that represent fractions of the total time for the animation and correspond to the position values.

SlideInView/SlideInView.m
```
CABasicAnimation *basic = [CABasicAnimation animationWithKeyPath:@"position"];
basic.fromValue = [NSValue valueWithCGPoint:fromPos];
basic.toValue = [NSValue valueWithCGPoint:toPos];
self.layer.position = toPos;
[self.layer addAnimation:basic forKey:@"basic"];
```

If the bounce option is set to NO, we use the simpler CABasicAnimation on the layer to achieve our slide-into position.

SlideInView/SlideInView.m
```
popInTimer = [NSTimer scheduledTimerWithTimeInterval:timer
                                              target:self
                                            selector:@selector(popIn)
                                            userInfo:nil
                                             repeats:NO];
```

Because we want the notification to be able to remove itself, we add an NSTimer object that calls the popIn method after the selected time.

SlideInView/SlideInView.m
```
[UIView beginAnimations:@"slideIn" context:nil];
self.frame = CGRectOffset(self.frame, -adjustX, -adjustY);
[UIView commitAnimations];
```

To dismiss the view, we don't need to worry about which animation style to use—we can use a UIView animation block to reposition the view offscreen. We simply use the negative value of the adjustment variables we calculated earlier to ensure we animate off the screen in the correct direction.

SlideInView/SlideInView.m
```
- (void)touchesBegan:(NSSet *)touches withEvent:(UIEvent *)event {
    [popInTimer invalidate];
    [self popIn];
}
```

A single touch to the SlideInView, which then triggers the touchesBegan:withEvent delegate method, is enough for us to cancel the timer and trigger the slide-back animation.

The MainViewController class shows the use of SlideInView objects from each of the four possible directions. The IBSlideIn instance was built in Interface Builder and shows how you can create more interesting, and possibly dynamic, notifications using multi-element views.

You can easily modify this technique to use different transition effects such as fades or flips or perhaps increase the visibility of the notification with additional animation in the view itself.

Recipe 4

Create Reusable Toggle Buttons

Problem

You want to create a custom button that can be toggled between an "on" and "off" state, and UISwitch doesn't quite fit your design. You want this button to be reusable, without the need to write state management code in every view controller that uses it.

Solution

The UIButton class is extremely versatile, making it relatively easy to implement this feature with a small amount of customization. As a subclass of UIControl, UIButton supports multiple states including highlighted, enabled, and selected. We can set custom images, text, and text colors for all of these states. This flexibility gives us all we need to add toggle support to a standard UIButton.

Let's take a look at what needs to be done. We need three button images: normal (or "off"), selected (or "on"), and a darker "pressed" mode. Figure 9, *An image-based toggle button*, on page 22 illustrates what these three states might look like. To make the process of supporting these states easier, and even automated, we'll declare a subclass. This PRPToggleButton will take care of all the state and image management for us, so we don't have to litter our controller code with image names and text colors every time a button is tapped. We can even set up the button in Interface Builder (IB), which allows the setting of per-state images, text, and colors.

The subclass declaration is very simple: it declares a boolean property to control whether the button automatically toggles itself when tapped, and it declares a convenience method for setting up and managing the various button state images.

ToggleButton/Classes/PRPToggleButton.h
```
@interface PRPToggleButton : UIButton {}

// Defaults to YES
@property (nonatomic, getter=isOn) BOOL on;
@property (nonatomic, getter=isAutotoggleEnabled) BOOL autotoggleEnabled;
```

A demonstration of our PRPToggleButton in its off, on, and highlighted (finger down) states

Figure 9—An image-based toggle button

```
+ (id)buttonWithOnImage:(UIImage *)onImage
              offImage:(UIImage *)offImage
       highlightedImage:(UIImage *)highlightedImage;

- (BOOL)toggle;
```

@end

Since most toggle buttons tend to be image-based, we create a convenience method that abstracts redundant calls to -setBackgroundImage:forState:; therefore, our controller code does less work and has fewer potential bugs. It stores the "on" and "off" images in properties, to be used based on the corresponding button state.

ToggleButton/Classes/PRPToggleButton.m
```
+ (id)buttonWithOnImage:(UIImage *)onImage
              offImage:(UIImage *)offImage
       highlightedImage:(UIImage *)highlightedImage {
```

```
    PRPToggleButton *button;
    button = [self buttonWithType:UIButtonTypeCustom];
    button.onImage = onImage;
    button.offImage = offImage;
    [button setBackgroundImage:offImage forState:UIControlStateNormal];
    [button setBackgroundImage:highlightedImage
                    forState:UIControlStateHighlighted];
    button.autotoggleEnabled = YES;
    return button;
}
```

Note the autotoggle behavior is explicitly set to YES, since BOOL ivars default to NO.

We perform autotoggling by peeking into UIControl's standard construct for tracking touch events. We do this to find out when the button has received a proper tap; the built-in control logic remains unchanged.

ToggleButton/Classes/PRPToggleButton.m
```
- (void)endTrackingWithTouch:(UITouch *)touch withEvent:(UIEvent *)event {
    [super endTrackingWithTouch:touch withEvent:event];
    if (self.touchInside && self.autotoggleEnabled) {
        [self toggle];
    }
}
```

The -toggle method flips the button's on property as a convenience; the real work is done in the -setOn: accessor method. This is where we switch the default background image based on the managed on/off state.

ToggleButton/Classes/PRPToggleButton.m
```
- (BOOL)toggle {
    self.on = !self.on;
    return self.on;
}
```

ToggleButton/Classes/PRPToggleButton.m
```
- (void)setOn:(BOOL)onBool {
    if (on != onBool) {
        on = onBool;
        [self setBackgroundImage:(on ? self.onImage : self.offImage)
                    forState:UIControlStateNormal];
    }
}
```

Adding IB support to this class is trivial. Since IB uses an archiver to load its objects from the nib, the code in +buttonWithOnImage:OffImage: is never executed. So, we implement the -awakeFromNib method to properly initialize the autotoggle behavior.

ToggleButton/Classes/PRPToggleButton.m

```
- (void)awakeFromNib {
    self.autotoggleEnabled = YES;
    self.onImage = [self backgroundImageForState:UIControlStateSelected];
    self.offImage = [self backgroundImageForState:UIControlStateNormal];
    [self setBackgroundImage:nil forState:UIControlStateSelected];
}
```

Using the toggle button from Interface Builder is now a snap. We just drag a Button object from the Library into our parent view, select the Identity inspector, and enter PRPToggleButton as the button's class. If the class name does not autocomplete this as we type, it's possible the class was not found. We'll know for sure when we run the project: if we see Unknown class PRPToggle-Button in Interface Builder file in the console, then either the class is missing from the compiled application or its name does not match what we entered in the Custom Class field. We need to check our spelling in both places. Figure 10, *Using PRPToggleButton in Interface Builder*, on page 25 shows this XIB configuration in Xcode 4.

Once we've configured the class identity, we select the Attributes inspector, where we set our on, off, and highlighted images for the Selected, Default, and Highlighted State Configurations, respectively. There is a small amount of trickery here. Our PRPToggleButton merely switches two images in and out of the Normal control state, but we need a place to put the "on" image in IB. We temporarily use the Selected state for this and then clean up after ourselves in -awakeFromNib. Take another look at that code to see how it works.

Run the application, and note that toggling is handled automatically; you need to add a target and action only if your application logic needs to respond to state changes as they happen. You can check the button's on property at any time to find out its toggle state.

That's it! We now have built-in, reusable toggle support for any application, from code or nib. If we were using a standard UIButton, we'd have to include a significant amount of management code in every view controller that wanted to do this. With all this logic factored away in our custom button, our controller code becomes much cleaner.

ToggleButton/Classes/ToggleButtonViewController.m

```
self.toggleButton = [PRPToggleButton buttonWithOnImage:self.buttonOnImage
                                              offImage:self.buttonOffImage
                                       highlightedImage:highlightedImage];
CGFloat buttonWidth = self.buttonOnImage.size.width;
CGFloat buttonHeight = self.buttonOffImage.size.height;
self.toggleButton.frame = CGRectMake(kButtonX, 100.0, buttonWidth, buttonHeight);
[self.view addSubview:toggleButton];
```

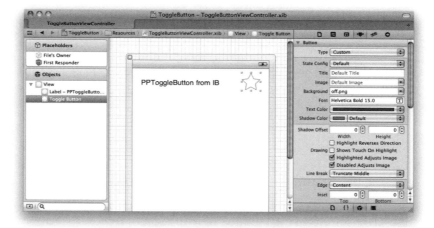

PRPToggleButton uses the standard button states and background images to manage its on/off state, so we can set those right from IB. Remember to set the custom class in the Identity inspector, or you'll end up with a plain UIButton.

Figure 10—Using PRPToggleButton in Interface Builder

Responding to taps on PRPToggleButton is the same as it would be for any other button: just add a target/action in your code, or from IB, and do whatever is appropriate after checking the on property.

```
ToggleButton/Classes/ToggleButtonViewController.m
- (IBAction)toggleButtonTapped:(id)sender {
    if ([sender isOn]) {
        NSLog(@"Toggle button was activated!");
    } else {
        NSLog(@"Toggle button was deactivated!");
    }
}
```

Be sure to look at the accompanying UIButton-based implementation alongside this code in -[ToggleButtonViewController viewDidLoad] and -[ToggleButtonViewController plainButtonTapped:] to see the how much effort is saved. Not only are we doing less work with PRPToggleButton, but the controller's role is now clearer: the action code merely responds to the state change, rather than manages it.

Recipe 5

Form Rounded Views with Textured Colors

Problem

The UIView subclasses, buttons, and labels you use look a little dull, and you want to add some texture to the background—ideally with rounded edges and a border.

Solution

In iOS all UIViews are *layer-backed*—meaning that a view or subview is built on its own hardware-based layer. This is great for performance because you can reposition, resize, and transform views, without having to redraw them. But you can also directly manipulate the properties of a view's underlying layer for greater access to the inner workings of the view.

Each UIView, or subclass, exposes a layer property that is the read-only reference to its underlying layer, but all the properties of that layer can be modified. The CALayer properties of interest here include backgroundColor, borderWidth, borderColor, and cornerRadius. Setting any of these on the CALayer of any subview of UIView has a direct impact on the presentation of the view (see Figure 11, *Rounded views with texture*, on page 27).

We can't get the desired look—textured, with rounded edges and a border—simply by setting the backgroundColor of the layer; for that we need to use the UIColor class method colorWithPatternImage:, which creates a repeating pattern from any image. We do need to pick the images carefully, though; otherwise, the joins in the repeats are too obvious. To avoid this problem, we can use a larger image, perhaps closer in size to the view we plan to use it with. This is especially important if we are using the pattern for the backgroundColor property, because we will effectively be setting a background image for the view. This is really easy to use because it's still a UIColor, so any method or property that expects a UIColor object will gladly accept the patterned image.

After creating our set of patterned colors, we instantiate a normal UIButton object. We then modify the layer properties we need to give the desired effect, setting the cornerRadius to give a rounded rectangle with an 8-point border width and using the patterned colors for the borderColor and the backgroundColor.

Figure 11—Rounded views with texture

Setting up target/action pairs for the TouchDown and TouchUpInside events, with alternate values for the borderColor and cornerRadius properties, gives clear feedback to the user that the button has been touched.

RoundedView/Classes/RoundedViewViewController.m

```
// Defining the Textured colors from UIImages

thickColor =    [UIColor colorWithPatternImage:
                [UIImage imageNamed:@"thickColorGradient.png"]];
UIColor *grayGradient = [UIColor colorWithPatternImage:
                        [UIImage imageNamed:@"grayGradient.png"]];
UIColor *steelColor =   [UIColor colorWithPatternImage:
                        [UIImage imageNamed:@"simpleSteel.png"]];
UIColor *steelTexture = [UIColor colorWithPatternImage:
                        [UIImage imageNamed:@"steelTexture.png"]];
UIColor *woodTexture =  [UIColor colorWithPatternImage:
                        [UIImage imageNamed:@"woodTexture.png"]];

CGRect buttonFrame = CGRectMake(60, 60, 200,80);
UIButton *roundButton = [[UIButton alloc] initWithFrame:buttonFrame];
roundButton.layer.borderWidth = 8;
roundButton.layer.borderColor = thickColor.CGColor;
```

```
roundButton.layer.backgroundColor = grayGradient.CGColor;
roundButton.layer.cornerRadius = roundButton.bounds.size.height/4;
[self.view addSubview:roundButton];

[roundButton addTarget:self action:@selector(buttonPressed:)
    forControlEvents:UIControlEventTouchDown];
[roundButton addTarget:self action:@selector(buttonReleased:)
    forControlEvents:UIControlEventTouchUpInside |
UIControlEventTouchUpOutside];
```

Here we are using a UIView with a UILabel subview. The view's layer is manipulated like the button earlier to give an interesting background for the label.

RoundedView/Classes/RoundedViewViewController.m
```
UILabel *labelA = [self centeredLabel:buttonFrame label:@"Colorful"];
labelA.font = [UIFont fontWithName:@"MarkerFelt-Thin" size:36];
labelA.textColor = thickColor;
[roundButton addSubview:labelA];

CGRect viewFrame = CGRectMake(30, 210, 260, 50);
UIView *steelView = [[UIView alloc] initWithFrame:viewFrame];
steelView.layer.borderWidth = 5;
steelView.layer.borderColor = steelColor.CGColor;
steelView.layer.backgroundColor = steelTexture.CGColor;
steelView.layer.cornerRadius = steelView.bounds.size.height/4;
[self.view addSubview:steelView];

UILabel *labelB = [self centeredLabel:viewFrame label:@"Brushed Steel"];
labelB.font = [UIFont fontWithName:@"TrebuchetMS-Bold" size:28];
labelB.textColor = steelColor;
[steelView addSubview:labelB];
```

We could go even further and modify the same properties directly on the UILabel's layer to achieve the same effect.

RoundedView/Classes/RoundedViewViewController.m
```
CGRect labelFrame = CGRectMake(10, 340, 300, 40);
UILabel *label = [self centeredLabel:labelFrame
                                label:@"A Much Longer Label"];
label.frame = labelFrame;
label.font = [UIFont fontWithName:@"Thonburi-Bold" size:24];
label.textColor = steelColor;
label.shadowColor = [UIColor blackColor];
label.layer.borderWidth = 4;
label.layer.borderColor = steelColor.CGColor;
label.layer.backgroundColor = woodTexture.CGColor;
label.layer.cornerRadius = label.frame.size.height/2;
[self.view addSubview:label];
```

Other properties are exposed by the CALayer class that are not available to the UIView class, so it's well worth checking out the iOS documentation to see what other interesting effects you can achieve.

Recipe 6

Put Together a Reusable Web View

Problem

Some of the most elegant and customized native apps on the market still rely on web content now and then, if only to open a URL without punting to Safari. UIWebView is an elegant class that's easy to use, but there's a decent amount of support code that goes into displaying even a single web page.

Solution

We can save ourselves time and effort over multiple projects by making a basic web view that's displayable either modally or as part of a navigation stack. The controller takes a URL from the calling code and automatically loads the content when the view is loaded. It displays an activity indicator view while the page loads, and it performs a smooth transition once the content is ready to be displayed. We fire up this controller, display it with just a few lines of code, then get back to more important business. Figure 12, *A reusable web view controller*, on page 30 shows this view in action.

The PRPWebViewController class creates a basic, resizable root view containing a UIWebView for displaying web content and creates a large white UIActivityIndicatorView to tell the user that content is loading. We create the hierarchy in code so we don't need to move a xib file every time we reuse this class.

The activity indicator is centered within the main view at load time, and all of the Margin autoresizing masks are set to ensure it will stay centered whenever the main view is resized or rotated.

SmartWebView/PRPWebViewController.m
```
activityIndicator.autoresizingMask = UIViewAutoresizingFlexibleTopMargin |
                                     UIViewAutoresizingFlexibleRightMargin |
                                     UIViewAutoresizingFlexibleBottomMargin |
                                     UIViewAutoresizingFlexibleLeftMargin;
CGRect aiFrame = self.activityIndicator.frame;
CGFloat originX = (self.view.bounds.size.width - aiFrame.size.width) / 2;
CGFloat originY = (self.view.bounds.size.height - aiFrame.size.height) / 2;
aiFrame.origin.x = floorl(originX);
aiFrame.origin.y = floorl(originY);
self.activityIndicator.frame = aiFrame;
```

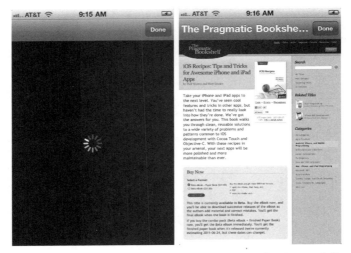

Our web view controller initially shows an activity indicator and then fades
the web content on-screen when it's loaded.

Figure 12—A reusable web view controller

We flatten the calculated origin to avoid nonintegral coordinates, which can
blur a view's appearance.

Our controller implements the standard UIWebViewDelegate methods to detect
when the request is finished. If the load was successful, it hides the activity
indicator and fades the web view on-screen. This gives a smoother transition
while the user waits for content to appear. The controller also pulls the title
element from the loaded HTML and sets that as its navigation title.

SmartWebView/PRPWebViewController.m

```
- (void)webViewDidFinishLoad:(UIWebView *)wv {
    [self.activityIndicator stopAnimating];
    [self fadeWebViewIn];
    if (self.title == nil) {
        NSString *docTitle = [self.webView
            stringByEvaluatingJavaScriptFromString:@"document.title;"];
        if ([docTitle length] > 0) {
            self.navigationItem.title = docTitle;
        }
    }
    SEL sel_didFinishLoading = @selector(webControllerDidFinishLoading:);
    if ([self.delegate respondsToSelector:sel_didFinishLoading]) {
        [self.delegate webControllerDidFinishLoading:self];
    }
}
```

When Does a Web View Really Finish Loading?

Depending on the content you load, UIWebView can be a bit unpredictable. If the page you request contains iframes or dynamic content, your code may receive multiple webViewDidFinishLoad: messages. Because every individual use case may have a different definition of "finished," this recipe does not do anything to audit or monitor these multiple callbacks. You're free to tailor the class to your specific needs.

Note that if the view controller's title property was already set, the code respects that. So if you're using PRPWebViewController and you want a static navigation title rather than one based on the web content, just set the title property on the view controller when you create it.

A backgroundColor property is also exposed for easy customization of the view's appearance while loading.

SmartWebView/PRPWebViewController.m
```
- (void)setBackgroundColor:(UIColor *)color {
    if (backgroundColor != color) {
        [backgroundColor release];
        backgroundColor = [color retain];
        [self resetBackgroundColor];
    }
}
```

Why create a special property for the background color? Why not just set it on the view directly? Because depending on when we do that, we might force the view to load prematurely. The resetBackgroundColor method sets the color only if and when the view is loaded. Calling this method from setBackgroundColor: and viewDidLoad respects both the caller's wishes and UIKit's lazy loading mechanics.

SmartWebView/PRPWebViewController.m
```
- (void)resetBackgroundColor {
    if ([self isViewLoaded]) {
        UIColor *bgColor = self.backgroundColor;
        if (bgColor == nil) {
            bgColor = [UIColor whiteColor];
        }
        self.view.backgroundColor = bgColor;
    }
}
```

There's also a convenient BOOL property that generates a system Done button, which is useful when presenting the controller modally. Bar button items are among those things we create all the time but are rather verbose; in this case, we've packaged one inside our reusable controller.

SmartWebView/PRPWebViewController.m

```
- (void)setShowsDoneButton:(BOOL)shows {
    if (showsDoneButton != shows) {
        showsDoneButton = shows;
        if (showsDoneButton) {
            UIBarButtonItem *done = [[UIBarButtonItem alloc]
                initWithBarButtonSystemItem:UIBarButtonSystemItemDone
                                     target:self
                                     action:@selector(doneButtonTapped:)];
            self.navigationItem.rightBarButtonItem = done;
            [done release];
        } else {
            self.navigationItem.rightBarButtonItem = nil;
        }
    }
}
```

To do all this work on our behalf, PRPWebViewController needs to act as the web view's delegate. But what if our code cares about a load failure or needs to know when the page finished loading? Delegation is a "one-to-one" relationship, so we can't just steal the UIWebViewDelegate role from PRPWebViewController or we'll break its functionality. So in this case, we'll declare a new PRPWebViewControllerDelegate delegate to echo relevant events to an interested party.

SmartWebView/PRPWebViewControllerDelegate.h

```
@class PRPWebViewController;

@protocol PRPWebViewControllerDelegate <NSObject>

@optional
- (void)webControllerDidFinishLoading:(PRPWebViewController *)controller;

- (void)webController:(PRPWebViewController *)controller
 didFailLoadWithError:(NSError *)error;

- (BOOL)webController:(PRPWebViewController *)controller
shouldAutorotateToInterfaceOrientation:(UIInterfaceOrientation)orientation;
@end
```

The autorotation method allows you to dictate the controller's behavior based on your own UI. All of these protocol methods are optional: you have no responsibility to implement any of them. The PRPWebViewController can still act completely on its own.

You now have a self-sufficient web view that presents a smooth transition to users as its content loads. All you need to do to include web content in your apps is create a PRPWebViewController, set a URL, and display it.

Customize Sliders and Progress Views

Problem

The standard look of UISlider and UIProgressViews may not match the rest of your app. Unfortunately, Interface Builder allows you to adjust only the width. What can you do to give these elements a different look?

Solution

To go beyond the basics, we need to dip into code to explore some of the available image properties and understand how to use stretchable UIImages.

UISlider has a set of properties that aren't exposed by Interface Builder: currentMaximumTrackImage, currentMinimumTrackImage, and currentThumbImage. These properties give a lot of flexibility by letting us specify alternate images for the control. To get the most out of them, we need to understand how stretchable UIImages work (see Figure 13, *Custom slider demo screen*, on page 34).

We create a stretchable UIImage from an image file just like any other image, but we must also set the leftCapWidth and topCapHeight values. We do this by calling the stretchableImageWithLeftCapWidth:topCapHeight method to define the length of the sections that will remain unstretched. If an image is 100 points in width and we define the leftCapWidth as 49, then the 50th point would be the one that is stretched (or duplicated), and the remaining 50 points would remain fixed. If we then set the image length to 200, then 150 copies of the stretched point are inserted to fill out the image. As you can see, we need to pick the image and stretch points carefully so it still looks correct when it is stretched. Check out the images in the sample code. The images appear to be oddly shaped but achieve the look we want when they are stretched.

CustomSlider/Classes/CustomSliderViewController.m
```
UIImage* sunImage = [UIImage imageNamed:@"sun.png"];
[customSlider setThumbImage:sunImage forState:UIControlStateNormal];
```

We can use the thumbImage property to set a new image for the draggable element of the slider. In this case, the *sun* image looks quite striking compared to the default white dot but also serves to hide the join between the two track images.

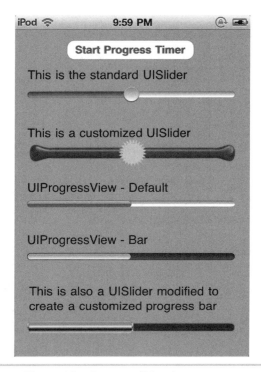

Figure 13—Custom slider demo screen

CustomSlider/Classes/CustomSliderViewController.m
```
customProgress.userInteractionEnabled = NO;

UIImage* sliderPoint = [UIImage imageNamed:@"sliderPoint.png"];
[customProgress setThumbImage:sliderPoint forState:UIControlStateNormal];

UIImage *leftStretch = [[UIImage imageNamed:@"leftImage.png"]
                              stretchableImageWithLeftCapWidth:10.0
                                                  topCapHeight:0.0];
[customProgress setMinimumTrackImage:leftStretch
                              forState:UIControlStateNormal];

UIImage *rightStretch = [[UIImage imageNamed:@"rightImage.png"]
                              stretchableImageWithLeftCapWidth:10.0
                                                  topCapHeight:0.0];
[customProgress setMaximumTrackImage:rightStretch
                              forState:UIControlStateNormal];
```

We are not creating a true UIProgressView here but instead are using a partly disabled slider to achieve the same effect and in so doing gain the ability to use the same styling technique as for the UISlider. A subtle element here is that the image we use for the thumb image is much smaller and effectively acts as an end cap for the end of the minimum track image. With the userInteractionEnabled property set to NO and no obvious draggable element present, the slider appears to be a stylized progress bar.

The demo app includes a timer, activated by the button at the top of the screen, to demonstrate how you can easily create an animated progress bar by modifying the value property of the UISlider.

Recipe 8

Shape a Custom Gesture Recognizer

Problem

Apple provides a set of basic gesture recognizers, but what if you want to go further and recognize something more complex?

Solution

Introduced by Apple with iOS 3.2, gesture recognizers provide the best solution for all your touch recognition needs. They are easy to use, and you don't have to write any of the tedious code usually required to track the various stages of touch input. You have recognizers at your disposal for all of the basic gestures: tap, pinch, rotate, swipe, pan, and long press. But to go further and recognize something more complex, like a circle, you need to build a custom gesture recognizer.

We base our new class, PRPCircleGestureRecognizer, on the abstract class UIGestureRecognizer, but we need to include UIKit/UIGestureRecognizerSubclass.h, because this declares additional methods and properties we may need. We also need to decide whether to make our gesture recognizer discrete or continuous. A discrete recognizer triggers the delegate action only when the gesture has been fully recognized, whereas the continuous gesture triggers the delegate action for each of the touch events that it considers to be valid.

Choosing the appropriate recognizer type depends on how we want to recognize a circle. Each touch point must lie close to the circumference, allowing for a defined amount of deviation. Unfortunately, neither the center point nor the radius of the circle is defined; therefore, the position of the circumference is unknown. To solve this problem, each of the touch points must be stored until the gesture is completed so that the extreme points of the gesture can be used to calculate the diameter and, from that, establish the position of the center point and radius. A circle gesture recognizer, therefore, must be discrete, because it can validate the touch points only once the user gesture has been completed.

The base class handles all touches and makes the required callbacks to the delegate action, so we must include a call to Super in each of the delegate methods we implement. Equally important is the underlying state machine that the base class monitors to track the recognition process. For a discrete recognizer, the state property can be set to only one of these valid states: [1]

- UIGestureRecognizerStatePossible

- UIGestureRecognizerStateRecognized

- UIGestureRecognizerStateFailed

UIGestureRecognizerStatePossible is the initial state and indicates that the recognition process is ongoing. If recognition succeeds, then the state property will be set to UIGestureRecognizerStateRecognized, and the delegate action selector will be called. If, at any point, a touch point is found outside the calculated bounds of the circle, the state property will be set to UIGestureRecognizerStateFailed, triggering a call to the reset method to reinitialize the process and wait for a new touch sequence.

CircleGestureRecognizer/PRPCircleGestureRecognizer.m
```
- (void)touchesBegan:(NSSet *)touches withEvent:(UIEvent *)event {
        [super touchesBegan:touches withEvent:event];
        if ([self numberOfTouches] != 1) {
                self.state = UIGestureRecognizerStateFailed;
                return;
        }
    self.points = [NSMutableArray array];
    CGPoint touchPoint = [[touches anyObject] locationInView:self.view];
    lowX = touchPoint;
    lowY = lowX;
    if (self.deviation == 0) self.deviation = 0.4;
    moved = NO;
}
```

The touchesBegan:withEvent: method acts as our initializer, and the mutable array, which will hold our stored touch points, is instantiated. The first touch point is then added, and the low X and Y values are set to the current point so that they can be used later in calculating the longest line. If the deviation property has not already been set, then a default value is assigned.

CircleGestureRecognizer/PRPCircleGestureRecognizer.m
```
- (void)touchesMoved:(NSSet *)touches withEvent:(UIEvent *)event {
        [super touchesMoved:touches withEvent:event];
        if ([self numberOfTouches] != 1) {
                self.state = UIGestureRecognizerStateFailed;
        }
```

---

1. A continuous recognizer actually requires more states. For the full list of states, refer to the iPad developer guide at Apple.com.

```
        if (self.state == UIGestureRecognizerStateFailed) return;

        CGPoint touchPoint = [[touches anyObject] locationInView:self.view];

        if (touchPoint.x > highX.x) highX = touchPoint;
        else if (touchPoint.x < lowX.x) lowX = touchPoint;
        if (touchPoint.y > highY.y) highY = touchPoint;
        else if (touchPoint.y < lowY.y) lowY = touchPoint;
        [self.points addObject:[NSValue valueWithCGPoint:touchPoint]];
        moved = YES;
}
```

The touchesMoved:withEvent: method is called for each point tracked. Multiple touches are considered invalid, and if these are identified, the state property is set to UIGestureRecognizerStateFailed. At this stage, because the circumference is not yet known, the touch point cannot yet be validated, so it is added to the points array. To calculate the diameter, the outlying points on the x- and y-axes need to be established. If the touch point exceeds one of the currently stored outliers, its value is reset to the touch point. To avoid invalidly recognizing a single point as a circle, the moved Boolean is set to YES to indicate that the touchesMoved:withEvent: method has been called at least once.

CircleGestureRecognizer/PRPCircleGestureRecognizer.m
```
- (void)touchesEnded:(NSSet *)touches withEvent:(UIEvent *)event {
        [super touchesEnded:touches withEvent:event];
        if (self.state == UIGestureRecognizerStatePossible) {
                if (moved && [self recognizeCircle]) {
                        self.state = UIGestureRecognizerStateRecognized;
                } else {
                        self.state = UIGestureRecognizerStateFailed;
                }
        }
}
```

The touchesEnded:withEvent: method needs only to check that touches have moved, and then it calls the recognizedCircle method to perform the meat of the validation.

CircleGestureRecognizer/PRPCircleGestureRecognizer.m
```
- (BOOL) recognizeCircle {
    CGFloat tempRadius;
    CGPoint tempCenter;
    CGFloat xLength = distanceBetweenPoints(highX, lowX);
    CGFloat yLength = distanceBetweenPoints(highY, lowY);
    if (xLength > yLength) {
        tempRadius = xLength/2;
        tempCenter = CGPointMake(lowX.x + (highX.x-lowX.x)/2,
                                 lowX.y + (highX.y-lowX.y)/2);
    } else {
```

```
            tempRadius = yLength/2;
            tempCenter = CGPointMake(lowY.x + (highY.x-lowY.x)/2,
                                     lowY.y + (highY.y-lowY.y)/2);
    }
    CGFloat deviant = tempRadius * self.deviation;

    CGFloat endDistance =
    distanceBetweenPoints([[self.points objectAtIndex:0] CGPointValue],
                          [[self.points lastObject] CGPointValue]);
    if (endDistance > deviant*2) {
        return NO;
    }

    for (NSValue *pointValue in self.points) {
        CGPoint point = [pointValue CGPointValue];
        CGFloat pointRadius = distanceBetweenPoints(point, tempCenter);
        if (abs(pointRadius - tempRadius) > deviant) {
            return NO;
        }
    }
    self.radius = tempRadius;
    self.center = tempCenter;
    return YES;
}
```

The recognizedCircle method calculates the distance between the touch points stored in the outlier variables LowX, HighX, LowY, and highY, the longest of these being taken as the diameter. From this, the center point and radius are easily calculated. A deviant value is then calculated based on the radius and the deviation property. To ensure that a full circle was recognized, the first and last touch points must not be too far apart (twice the deviant value); if they are, the state property will be set to UIGestureRecognizerStateFailed. Each of the points in a points array is validated by ensuring that the distance between the point and the circle center point is not more or less than the radius plus or minus the deviant. If all our points are validated, then the radius and center properties are set, and the return value is set to YES, signifying success. The touchesEnded:withEvent: method then sets the state property to UIGestureRecognizerStateRecognized.

When successful, the base class code triggers a call to the delegate action selector, which is specified when the gesture recognizer is instantiated—in this case, the circleFound method in mainViewController.m. In our example here, a smiley face, sized to match the radius and position of the recognized circle, is drawn to the UIView that was attached to the recognizer.

Though the code here is specific to recognizing a circle gesture, you can easily adapt this technique to recognize any type of gesture that you require.

Recipe 9

Create Self-contained Alert Views

Problem

The UIAlertView class gives you an easy, consistent interface for presenting important information to your users. The logic for responding to user input in those views, however, can be cumbersome and error-prone. Wouldn't it be great to have a version of UIAlertView that is self-contained, easy to use, and easy to interact with from any controller code?

Solution

UIKit has a generous library of Apple-designed controls that are ready to use in any app, and UIAlertView is a great example: you get an Apple-designed dialog with a title, message, and buttons, and it even dims the screen to draw the user's attention to the alert.

Creating an alert is easy enough: you initialize it and call show, and Apple does the rest. If all you're doing is giving the user a message, with no action to be taken, this is a straightforward flow. If you present the user with choices, however, and need to respond to those choices, you have some more work to do: set your code as the alert view's delegate, and implement one or more of the UIAlertViewDelegate protocol methods such as -alertView:clickedButtonAtIndex:.

It's inside this delegate method where things can get not only cumbersome but dangerous. You need to determine which button was tapped in order to respond accordingly. But what's the best way? You have a few choices:

- Do a hard-coded comparison/switch against the button indexes

- Send -buttonTitleAtIndex to the alert view, and compare the strings

The buttonIndex passed to your delegate method isn't particularly useful, because you initially passed the button titles as varargs to the standard -initWithTitle:message:... method. Perhaps you've recorded the indices as constants elsewhere, but then you've introduced undesirable coupling into your code.

The second option—comparing button titles—is much less risky: provided you've defined the strings as globals or localized strings, the code should still work even after rearranging the button titles.

Either of these approaches carries some refactoring headaches and requires a nontrivial amount of scaffolding every time you want to throw up an alert view. It can get particularly ugly if your view controller presents multiple alerts based on the situation: now it's not just "which button," but "which button in which alert?"

`PRPAlertView/ScrapCode.m`
```objc
- (void)alertView:(UIAlertView *)alertView
      willDismissWithButtonIndex:(NSInteger)buttonIndex {
    NSString *buttonTitle = [alertView buttonTitleAtIndex:buttonIndex];
    if (alertView == self.offlineAlertView) {
        if ([buttonTitle isEqualToString:PRPOKTitle]) {
            // ...
        } else if ([buttonTitle isEqualToString:PRPCancelTitle]) {
            // ...
        }
    } else if (alertView == self.serverErrorAlertView) {
        if ([buttonTitle isEqualToString:PRPTryAgainTitle]) {
            // ...
        }
    }
}
```

The delegate model is well-established in Cocoa Touch, but we can make the whole process much nicer with the help of blocks. We're going to create a subclass, PRPAlertView, that streamlines the process of presenting alerts. Afterwords, you'll have a reusable component that does in one method what used to require three or four. By using blocks, we can sidestep the delegate code and define the desired behavior for each button at creation time—not later, when the context of which-button-in-which-alert has been lost.

The subclass interface is very simple. We've avoided any initialization or delegates and used class methods that show alerts immediately. The first method takes a "cancel" or default button title, one other button title, and respective blocks to invoke when each button is tapped. We also define a simple block type (no return, no arguments) to make the code more readable.

`PRPAlertView/PRPAlertView/PRPAlertView.h`
```objc
+ (void)showWithTitle:(NSString *)title
              message:(NSString *)message
          cancelTitle:(NSString *)cancelTitle
          cancelBlock:(PRPAlertBlock)cancelBlock
           otherTitle:(NSString *)otherTitle
           otherBlock:(PRPAlertBlock)otherBlock;
```

PRPAlertView/PRPAlertView/PRPAlertView.h

```
typedef void(^PRPAlertBlock)(void);
```

There's also a simplified "show and do nothing" convenience method for when you just need to tell the user something but no response is needed.

PRPAlertView/PRPAlertView/PRPAlertView.h

```
+ (void)showWithTitle:(NSString *)title
              message:(NSString *)message
          buttonTitle:(NSString *)buttonTitle;
```

The implementation is straightforward: both of these convenience methods create, show, and autorelease an alert using our newly defined -initWithTitle:... method listed next. This method saves the passed blocks and button titles into copy-style properties for comparison later. It also acts as its own delegate—if one or more of the handler blocks is actually passed.

PRPAlertView/PRPAlertView/PRPAlertView.m

```
+ (void)showWithTitle:(NSString *)title
              message:(NSString *)message
          cancelTitle:(NSString *)cancelTitle
          cancelBlock:(PRPAlertBlock)cancelBlk
           otherTitle:(NSString *)otherTitle
           otherBlock:(PRPAlertBlock)otherBlk {
    [[[[self alloc] initWithTitle:title message:message
                      cancelTitle:cancelTitle cancelBlock:cancelBlk
                       otherTitle:otherTitle otherBlock:otherBlk]
        autorelease] show];
}
```

PRPAlertView/PRPAlertView/PRPAlertView.m

```
- (id)initWithTitle:(NSString *)title
            message:(NSString *)message
        cancelTitle:(NSString *)cancelTitle
        cancelBlock:(PRPAlertBlock)cancelBlk
         otherTitle:(NSString *)otherTitle
         otherBlock:(PRPAlertBlock)otherBlk {

    if ((self = [super initWithTitle:title
                             message:message
                            delegate:self
                   cancelButtonTitle:cancelTitle
                   otherButtonTitles:otherTitle, nil])) {

        if (cancelBlk == nil && otherBlk == nil) {
            self.delegate = nil;
        }
        self.cancelButtonTitle = cancelTitle;
        self.otherButtonTitle = otherTitle;
        self.cancelBlock = cancelBlk;
```

```
        self.otherBlock = otherBlk;
    }
    return self;
}
```

The init method, as well as the properties, are tucked away in a private class extension to simplify the interface defined in the header file. This increases readability and encourages consumers to use only the convenience methods, which is the easiest way to use the class.

PRPAlertView/PRPAlertView/PRPAlertView.m
```
@interface PRPAlertView ()

@property (nonatomic, copy) PRPAlertBlock cancelBlock;
@property (nonatomic, copy) PRPAlertBlock otherBlock;
@property (nonatomic, copy) NSString *cancelButtonTitle;
@property (nonatomic, copy) NSString *otherButtonTitle;

- (id)initWithTitle:(NSString *)title
            message:(NSString *)message
        cancelTitle:(NSString *)cancelTitle
        cancelBlock:(PRPAlertBlock)cancelBlock
         otherTitle:(NSString *)otherTitle
         otherBlock:(PRPAlertBlock)otherBlock;

@end
```

The no-response-necessary convenience method just calls the same code with no handler blocks. The actual logic behind this class, then, is completely isolated.

PRPAlertView/PRPAlertView/PRPAlertView.h
```
+ (void)showWithTitle:(NSString *)title
              message:(NSString *)message
          buttonTitle:(NSString *)buttonTitle;
```

So, how do these blocks help us avoid the delegate? As you saw earlier, PRPAlertView acts as its own delegate and implements a UIAlertViewDelegate method internally to match up the blocks with their respective button titles.

PRPAlertView/PRPAlertView/PRPAlertView.m
```
- (void)alertView:(UIAlertView *)alertView
willDismissWithButtonIndex:(NSInteger)buttonIndex {
    NSString *buttonTitle = [alertView buttonTitleAtIndex:buttonIndex];
    if ([buttonTitle isEqualToString:self.cancelButtonTitle]) {
        if (self.cancelBlock) self.cancelBlock();
    } else if ([buttonTitle isEqualToString:self.otherButtonTitle]) {
        if (self.otherBlock) self.otherBlock();
    }
}
```

On Blocks and Retain Cycles

This recipe uses convenience methods that obscure the created UIAlertView—the initializer is hidden in a private class extension. This reinforces the concept that alerts are "temporary" elements and not really meant to stick around for very long. This concept is more important now that we're using blocks to handle the buttons, because *blocks retain any objects they reference*. Imagine your view controller references self from the cancelBlock passed to this class and then saves the alert in a property for future reuse. You'd then have a view controller retaining an alert view...which has a block property...which retains your view controller.

If your view controller is retained by the alert's block, it won't be deallocated until the retained alert (and therefore its block) is explicitly released. The alert, though, is stuck in a property on the view controller. This is called a *retain cycle*, and it can lead to serious memory leaks. We avoid this problem altogether by never exposing the autoreleased alert view we create so that nobody can retain it. Alert views are short-lived and inexpensive to allocate, so there should be no need to hold onto them.

You've probably noticed that this class allows only two buttons, which masks the UIAlertView support for a vararg list of "otherButtonTitles." This keeps the code simpler, and let's be honest: how many three-or-more-button alert views have you seen out there? If you think you need more than two buttons, you may well have a design problem to work out before you write any more code. That said, it's not too hard to add vararg support to this class (see Recipe 36, *Produce Intelligent Debug Output*, on page 176 for an example) and maintain the blocks and titles in a dictionary for easy lookup. We chose to keep it simple—both technically and aesthetically.

With PRPAlertView in place, the controller code becomes much simpler. Here's what we had to do before PRPAlertView to show a two-button alert with responses for each button:

PRPAlertView/ScrapCode.m
```objc
- (void)showAlert {
    UIAlertView *alert = [[UIAlertView alloc] initWithTitle:@"Uh Oh"
                                    message:@"Something bad happened."
                                    delegate:self
                        cancelButtonTitle:PRPAlertButtonTitleRunAway
                        otherButtonTitles:PRPAlertButtonTitleOnward, nil];
    [alert show];
    [alert release];
}
- (void)alertView:(UIAlertView *)alertView
        willDismissWithButtonIndex:(NSInteger)buttonIndex {
    NSString *buttonTitle = [alertView buttonTitleAtIndex:buttonIndex];
```

```
    if ([buttonTitle isEqualToString:PRPAlertButtonTitleAbort]) {
        [self runAway];
    } else if ([buttonTitle isEqualToString:PRPAlertButtonTitleOnward]) {
        [self proceedOnward];
    }
}
```

Here's how it looks with PRPAlertView:

PRPAlertView/ScrapCode.m

```
- (void)showAlert {
    [PRPAlertView showWithTitle:@"Uh Oh"
                        message:@"Something bad happened."
                    cancelTitle:PRPAlertButtonTitleAbort
                    cancelBlock:^(void) {
                        [self runAway];
                    }
                     otherTitle:PRPAlertButtonTitleOnward
                     otherBlock:^(void) {
                         [self proceedOnward];
                     }
    ];
}
```

With this recipe, we no longer have to worry about memory management, refactoring, coupling, or the complication of multiple interactive alerts that use the same controller. Everything the alert ever needs to do is defined in the very spot it's created. It removes the ambiguity of what code responds to the alert's buttons, which saves you and whoever inherits your code the trouble of finding where those old delegate methods might be living.

Recipe 10

Make a Label for Attributed Strings

Problem

The iOS label class cannot display an attributed string—that is, a string that contains "rich text" formats such as underline, colors, or mixed fonts.

Solution

When Apple added the Core Text APIs to iOS for lower-level text rendering, it also needed to include the NSAttributedString class, providing significantly more power for formatting text. Although OS X has the ability to render attributed strings through UI controls, iOS currently does not.

Core Text is a very deep API, dealing with glyphs and kerning, text runs, and lines, so it would be nice if you could solve this problem without having to dig too far.

Thankfully, Core Text does provide a very simple method that we can use to create a line of attributed text. We can then take that line and draw it into any graphics context (see Figure 14, *TableView of attributed labels*, on page 47). It makes sense to make our new class, PRPAttributedLabel, a UIView subclass because that provides the simplest way to get access to the graphics context we need.

The drawRect: method contains only three lines of code that deal directly with creating and rendering the attributed string. The majority of the code deals with fetching a reference to the context, saving and restoring the context state, and translating the context coordinates to match the inverted iOS coordinate system.

The first method, CTLineCreateWithAttributedString, creates a very simple Core Text line without the need for a typesetter object, because typesetting is done for us under the hood. We then set the position for the line within the frame of the view, using CGContextSetTextPosition. The current text position is in the center of the frame, so we need to calculate the offsets relative to that; in this simple case, we start at the left edge and move up one quarter of the frame's height from the bottom. None of this positioning takes into account

Figure 14—TableView of attributed labels

the attributes of the string, such as font size, so we will need to adjust our label frame size to fit the fonts used in our attributed strings. Just as with UILabel, it may take a little trial and error to get the lines to fit well.

Finally, we call the CTLineDraw method to draw the line into the graphics context at the specified point.

coreText/Classes/PRPAttributedLabel.m
```
- (void)drawRect:(CGRect)rect {
        if (self.attributedText == nil)
                return;
        CGContextRef context = UIGraphicsGetCurrentContext();
        CGContextSaveGState(context);
        CGContextTranslateCTM(context, self.bounds.size.width/2,
                                self.bounds.size.height);
        CGContextScaleCTM(context, 1.0, -1.0);
        CTLineRef line = CTLineCreateWithAttributedString((CFAttributedStringRef)
                                                self.attributedText);
        CGContextSetTextPosition(context, ceill(-self.bounds.size.width/2),
                                ceill(self.bounds.size.height/4));
        CTLineDraw(line, context);
        CGContextRestoreGState(context);
        CFRelease(line);
}
```

We are usually happy to let the @synthesize directive build our property setters for us, but in this case we need to make sure that any changes to the attributed string trigger a redraw so that the label is updated for every change. To do that, we need to create a customized setter for the attributedString property, which will contain the additional setNeedsDisplay call to force the redraw.

coreText/Classes/PRPAttributedLabel.m
```
- (void)setAttributedText:(NSAttributedString *)newAttributedText {
    if (attributedText != newAttributedText) {
        [attributedText release];
        attributedText = [newAttributedText copy];
        [self setNeedsDisplay];
    }
}
```

In the sample code we use a custom UITableViewController to show a list of available fonts. This is mostly boilerplate code, but in the tableView:cellForRowAtIndex: delegate method we replace the standard label with our PRPAttributedLabel. We set its size to match the full tableView width and height of the row.

coreText/Classes/FontsTableViewController.m
```
- (UITableViewCell *)tableView:(UITableView *)tableView
            cellForRowAtIndexPath:(NSIndexPath *)indexPath {

    static NSString *CellIdentifier = @"Cell";

    UITableViewCell *cell =
                    [tableView dequeueReusableCellWithIdentifier:CellIdentifier];
    if (cell == nil) {
        cell = [[[UITableViewCell alloc] initWithStyle:UITableViewCellStyleDefault
                                    reuseIdentifier:CellIdentifier] autorelease];
        CGRect frame = CGRectMake(10, 0, self.tableView.frame.size.width,
                                    self.tableView.rowHeight);
        PRPAttributedLabel *attLabel =
                            [[PRPAttributedLabel alloc] initWithFrame:frame];
        attLabel.backgroundColor = [UIColor whiteColor];
        attLabel.tag = 999;

        [cell.contentView addSubview:attLabel];
        [attLabel release];
    }

    PRPAttributedLabel *attLabel = (id)[cell.contentView viewWithTag:999];
    attLabel.attributedText =
                    [self.attributedFontNames objectAtIndex:indexPath.row];
    return cell;
}
```

There are many ways to create attributed strings—often they are built from retrieved XML data—but in this example we need a simple way to build some from normal strings so that we have something to display in our new label.

The illuminatedString method takes an input string and a font to create an attributed string, the first character of which will be set to be slightly larger and also bright red. The remainder of the string will be set to dark gray. We build up the string attribute by attribute, setting the colors and their ranges first and then adding the font with its various sizes.

coreText/Classes/FontsTableViewController.m
```
- (NSAttributedString *)illuminatedString:(NSString *)text
                                     font:(UIFont *)AtFont{

    int len = [text length];
    NSMutableAttributedString *mutaString =
    [[[NSMutableAttributedString alloc] initWithString:text] autorelease];
    [mutaString addAttribute:(NSString *)(kCTForegroundColorAttributeName)
                    value:(id)[UIColor darkGrayColor].CGColor
                    range:NSMakeRange(1, len-1)];
    [mutaString addAttribute:(NSString *)(kCTForegroundColorAttributeName)
                    value:(id)[UIColor redColor].CGColor
                    range:NSMakeRange(0, 1)];
    CTFontRef ctFont = CTFontCreateWithName((CFStringRef)AtFont.fontName,
                                            AtFont.pointSize,
                                            NULL);
    [mutaString addAttribute:(NSString *)(kCTFontAttributeName)
                    value:(id)ctFont
                    range:NSMakeRange(0, 1)];
    CTFontRef ctFont2 = CTFontCreateWithName((CFStringRef)AtFont.fontName,
                                            AtFont.pointSize*0.8,
                                            NULL);
    [mutaString addAttribute:(NSString *)(kCTFontAttributeName)
                    value:(id)ctFont2
                    range:NSMakeRange(1, len-1)];
    CFRelease(ctFont);
    CFRelease(ctFont2);
    return [[mutaString copy] autorelease];
}
```

The underlinedString method follows a very similar pattern but adds an underline attribute for the first six characters using the kCTUnderlineStyleSingle attribute identifier—again, a little artificial, but it demonstrates the effect quite nicely.

coreText/Classes/FontsTableViewController.m
```
[mutaString addAttribute:(NSString *)(kCTUnderlineStyleAttributeName)
                value:[NSNumber numberWithInt:kCTUnderlineStyleSingle]
                range:NSMakeRange(0, 6)];
```

As it stands, the PRPAttributedLabel class is not as fully featured as the UILabel class. If we wanted to enhance the features, to include better positioning options perhaps, we would need to dig further into Core Text to extract the line and glyph data. With that you could calculate the length and maximum height of the line, in points, and adjust the line positioning to allow for options such as centering or left/right alignment.

Scroll an Infinite Wall of Album Art

Problem

Scroll views are naturally constrained by the size of the view that is being scrolled. Scroll in any direction, and soon enough you'll hit the edge of the view and most likely bounce back. Currently, there is no easy way to make the contents of a UIScrollView wrap and still keep the feel of a continuous scroll.

Solution

Instead of hitting an edge, it would be nice to have the view wrap back around, for a more free-flowing experience. You could set up the scroll view to snap back to one edge as you reach the other, but this would create a visual jump and immediately stop any scrolling in progress. How then can you create an infinitely wrapping scroll view?

One option is to use a scroll view containing a *very* large view. If the view being scrolled is large enough, it will seem as if there are no boundaries at all. However, filling a huge view with enough data to give the impression of wrapping poses a problem with memory usage. When you write code for mobile devices, you have the constant need to preserve memory. Even with newer devices that have huge amounts of physical memory, multitasking requires you to consider your app footprint even when it's inactive.

What you need is a solution that instantiates a very large view and yet uses minimal memory—not quite as impossible as it sounds thanks to CATiledLayer, the class underlying the mapping APIs. Think of the Maps app as having the exact features you are looking for: seemingly endless scrolling and with the view filled with images on demand (see Figure 15, *Example of wall of album art*, on page 53).

The CATiledLayer class breaks up its contents into tiles of fixed size. As one of these tiles scrolls onto the display, it calls the drawRect method of the associated view with the rect parameter set to the size of the image to be drawn. This means that only the tiled areas that are currently visible, or about to be visible, need to be drawn, saving processing time and memory.

We are now a step closer to creating the continuous wrapping effect we are after. Because each tile is drawn in our drawRect method, we can control the image it contains. With a little math we can ensure that when we reach the end of the list of available images we simply start again with the first.

In this recipe we use a rich source of graphics data that is often overlooked: the iPod library. The only disadvantage is that the Xcode simulator does not give us access to the library, which means we need a little extra code to avoid an access error and to display an alternate image.

The MainViewController class contains the initialization code for the scroll view and an instance of our PRPTiledView class. The scroll view is our window into the tiled album view, so it just needs a frame no larger than the device window. Its contentsize, on the other hand, must be set to the size of the album view—in this case, a *very* large rect.

We want to steer clear of UIScrollViewDecelerationRateNormal—the default decelerationRate for a scroll view. While providing smooth, fast scrolling, it would cause a visible delay in the appearance of the album art, because the images would need to be constantly refreshed. By using UIScrollViewDecelerationRateFast instead, we can keep the scroll speed in check and ultimately provide a better user experience.

As cool as it is to have a huge virtual view, it would be completely pointless if the view started at the top-left corner, the default, because we would hit an edge almost immediately. So, we need to set the contentOffset property, our current distance from the top-left corner, to the center point of the view. With that set, we could literally scroll around for hours and still not hit a *real* edge. As with the contentsize, we need to set the frame size of the tiles view to the same very large rect.

InfiniteImages/MainViewController.m
```
- (void)viewDidLoad {
    [super viewDidLoad];

    width = self.view.bounds.size.width;
    height = self.view.bounds.size.height;
    CGRect frameRect = CGRectMake(0, 0, width, height);

    UIScrollView *infScroller = [[UIScrollView alloc]
                                         initWithFrame:frameRect];
    infScroller.contentSize = CGSizeMake(BIG, BIG);
    infScroller.delegate = self;
    infScroller.contentOffset = CGPointMake(BIG/2, BIG/2);
    infScroller.backgroundColor = [UIColor blackColor];
    infScroller.showsHorizontalScrollIndicator = NO;
```

Figure 15—Example of wall of album art

```
infScroller.showsVerticalScrollIndicator = NO;
infScroller.decelerationRate = UIScrollViewDecelerationRateFast;
[self.view addSubview:infScroller];
[infScroller release];

CGRect infFrame = CGRectMake(0, 0, BIG, BIG);
PRPTileView *tiles = [[PRPTileView alloc] initWithFrame:infFrame];

[infScroller addSubview:tiles];
[tiles release];
}
```

The PRPTiledView class is defined as a subclass of a standard UIView, but to make it a tiling view we need to set its backing layer class to be a CATiledLayer. In this case we actually use a subclass of CATiledLayer, for reasons we'll look at a bit later.

InfiniteImages/PRPTileView.m
```
+ (Class)layerClass {
    return [PRPTiledLayer class];
}
```

The initWithFrame: method needs to handle three tasks: setting the tile size, calculating the number of columns, and accessing the iTunes database to create an array of the available albums. We must take into account the possibility of a Retina Display being used on the target device, with its greatly increased resolution. So, we need to use the contentScaleFactor property to adjust the tile size, effectively doubling the size in this example. It is possible that an empty array will be returned from the MPMediaQuery call, but we will check for that later when we create the tile. If necessary, we can draw a placeholder image to fill the gap.

InfiniteImages/PRPTileView.m

```
- (id)initWithFrame:(CGRect)frame
{
    if ((self = [super initWithFrame:frame])) {
        PRPTiledLayer *tiledLayer = (PRPTiledLayer *)[self layer];
        CGFloat sf = self.contentScaleFactor;
        tiledLayer.tileSize = CGSizeMake(SIZE*sf, SIZE*sf);

        MPMediaQuery *everything = [MPMediaQuery albumsQuery];
        self.albumCollections = [everything collections];
    }
    return self;
}
```

The drawRect: method needs to calculate the exact column and row of the requested tile so that we can pass the position number to the tileAtPosition method. The image we get back from that call is then drawn directly into the specified rect of the tile layer.

InfiniteImages/PRPTileView.m

```
- (void)drawRect:(CGRect)rect {

    int col = rect.origin.x / SIZE;
    int row = rect.origin.y / SIZE;
    int columns = self.bounds.size.width/SIZE;
    UIImage *tile = [self tileAtPosition:row*columns+col];

    [tile drawInRect:rect];
}
```

The tileAtPosition method finds the index of the albumsCollections that we need by calculating the modulus of the position number and the number of albums. Using the representativeItem method, the MPMediaItem class returns a media item whose properties represent others in the collection. This ensures that we get a single image for each album in cases where there are differing images for each track.

The MPMediaItemArtwork class has a convenient method, imageWithSize:, that returns an instance of the album art at exactly the size we need, so we are not required to do any additional scaling of the image to fit the rect. Not all albums have art in the database, and in those cases we load a placeholder image to fill the rect.

InfiniteImages/PRPTileView.m
```
- (UIImage *)tileAtPosition:(int)position
{
    int albums = [self.albumCollections count];
    if (albums == 0) {
        return [UIImage imageNamed:@"missing.png"];
        }

    int index = position%albums;

    MPMediaItemCollection *mCollection = [self.albumCollections
                                        objectAtIndex:index];
    MPMediaItem *mItem = [mCollection representativeItem];
    MPMediaItemArtwork *artwork =
                [mItem valueForProperty: MPMediaItemPropertyArtwork];

    UIImage *image = [artwork imageWithSize: CGSizeMake(SIZE, SIZE)];
    if (!image) image = [UIImage imageNamed:@"missing.png"];

    return image;
}
```

We didn't use the CATiledLayer class earlier to override the layerClass of the view because of a slightly odd feature of the CATiledLayer API. Tiles are normally loaded on a background thread and fade into position over a set duration that defaults to 0.25 seconds. Oddly, fadeDuration is not a property; it is defined as a Class method, so it cannot be modified from the tile layer. To get around this, we need to create a CATiledLayer subclass, PRPTiledLayer, overriding the fadeDuration method, to return the value we want—in this case zero. This makes the new tiles appear immediately but ultimately has little effect on overall scrolling performance.

InfiniteImages/PRPTiledLayer.m
```
+ (CFTimeInterval)fadeDuration {
        return 0.00;
}
```

The final effect is quite satisfying, with the album art wrapping in all directions without any impact on the responsiveness of scrolling. Rapid scrolling causes images to lag behind a little, a side effect of using the tiled layer, but in general performance is quite acceptable, even on Retina Display devices.

Recipe 12

Play Tracks from a Wall of Album Art

Problem

You've used scroll views and tile layers to create a colorful wall of album art that wraps in all directions. Now you want to select just one of the albums and play some of the music from it. What do you need to do to extend Recipe 11, *Scroll an Infinite Wall of Album Art*, on page 51?

Solution

In the previous recipe, we explored scroll views and tile layers but mostly used the album art from the iPod library to provide an attractive visual background. You can do a lot more with the iPod library than just grab art; you can build a playlist of songs, play and control songs, and access the rich supply of metadata (see Figure 16, *iPod playback control*, on page 57).

Our first task is to modify the previous code so that we can detect which album has been selected. The simplest way to do that is to use a UITapGestureRecognizer. We can add this in the MainViewController and then call the new tapDetected method using the initWithTarget:action: method. We could add the recognizer to several views, but by adding it to the tiles view, the touch location that is returned to us is based on the coordinate system for that view, which makes it much easier for us to work out which album was selected.

We will put most of the iPod library code in a new controller class, PRPMusicViewController, so we create an instance of that, musicController, and set up its frame as centered on the current view.

InfinitePlayback/MainViewController.m
```
UITapGestureRecognizer *tap = [[UITapGestureRecognizer alloc]
                                    initWithTarget:self
                                    action:@selector(tapDetected:)];
[tiles addGestureRecognizer:tap];
[tap release];
musicController = [[PRPMusicViewController alloc]
                    initWithNibName:@"PRPMusicControllerView" bundle:nil];
CGFloat xPos = (width-musicController.view.frame.size.width)/2;
CGFloat yPos = (height-musicController.view.frame.size.height)/2;
musicController.view.frame = CGRectOffset(musicController.view.frame, xPos, yPos);
```

Figure 16—iPod playback control

We mainly use the tapDetected method as a toggle to show or hide the music controller. In this simple example, when the music controller is hidden, we also stop the music. We could let the music play on, but because the controller has already been dismissed, there is no way to control the music that is currently playing. Before we can present the music controller, we need to work out which album was selected. We call the collectionFromTouch method in the PRPTileView class to convert the touch point into an MPMediaItemCollection item. We can then set the mCollection property to a new playlist of all the tracks in this album.

Because we are adding our musicController view as a subview of the main view, the viewWillAppear: method will not be activated after it is loaded, so we need to call it manually here to complete our playback initialization.

InfinitePlayback/MainViewController.m
```
- (void)tapDetected:(UITapGestureRecognizer *)tap {
    PRPTileView *tiles = (PRPTileView *)tap.view;
    if (showingAlbum) {
        [musicController ZoomOutView];
```

```
        [musicController.myPlayer stop];
        showingAlbum = NO;
    } else {
        CGPoint tapPoint = [tap locationInView:tiles];
        MPMediaItemCollection *mCollection = [tiles
                                    collectionFromTouch:tapPoint];
        musicController.mCollection = [MPMediaItemCollection
                                collectionWithItems:[mCollection items]];
        [musicController viewWillAppear:NO];
        [self.view addSubview:musicController.view];
        [musicController ZoomInView];
        showingAlbum = YES;
    }
}
```

The collectionFromTouch method takes the touchPoint we detected, works out the position in the CATiledLayer, and from there calculates the index into the array of albumCollections. We can then pass the MPMediaItemCollection object, which contains the tracks of the album, back to the calling code.

InfinitePlayback/PRPTileView.m
```
- (MPMediaItemCollection *)collectionFromTouch:(CGPoint)touchPoint {
    int col = touchPoint.x / SIZE;
    int row = touchPoint.y / SIZE;
    int position = row*columns+col;
    int index = position%albums;

    MPMediaItemCollection *mCollection = [self.albumCollections
                                        objectAtIndex:index];
    return mCollection;
}
```

In the viewDidLoad method of our new PRPMusicViewController class we need to create an instance of the MPMusicPlayerController, the object that allows us to control playback of music from the iPod library. We also need to register for the iPod music player notifications, which are essential to allow us to respond to changes made by the MPMusicPlayerController itself, such as playing the next track in a playlist or stopping play at the end of an album. In those cases, we want to respond by changing the track information in the display or switching the playback button image.

InfinitePlayback/PRPMusicViewController.m
```
- (void)viewDidLoad
{
    [super viewDidLoad];
    myPlayer = [[MPMusicPlayerController applicationMusicPlayer] retain];
    NSNotificationCenter *notificationCenter = [NSNotificationCenter
                                                defaultCenter];
    [notificationCenter
```

```
    addObserver: self
    selector:    @selector (playingItemChanged:)
    name:        MPMusicPlayerControllerNowPlayingItemDidChangeNotification
    object:      myPlayer];

  [notificationCenter
   addObserver: self
   selector:    @selector (playbackStateChanged:)
   name:        MPMusicPlayerControllerPlaybackStateDidChangeNotification
   object:      myPlayer];

  [myPlayer beginGeneratingPlaybackNotifications];
}
```

In the viewWillAppear: method, we need to extract the album art again and set it as the background for our controller. In the XIB file for this view controller we have a small view hierarchy that places the album art under a semitransparent image of the classic CD case, with the playback controls added on top. We need to set the playback queue to be the full list of tracks for this album, and, in this simple case, we automatically play the first track.

InfinitePlayback/PRPMusicViewController.m

```
- (void) viewWillAppear:(BOOL)animated {
    [super viewWillAppear:animated];
    MPMediaItem *mItem = [self.mCollection representativeItem];
    MPMediaItemArtwork *artwork =
    [mItem valueForProperty: MPMediaItemPropertyArtwork];
    UIImage *image = [artwork imageWithSize: CGSizeMake(280, 280)];
    if (!image) image = [UIImage imageNamed:@"missing.png"];
    self.albumCover.image = image;
    [myPlayer setQueueWithItemCollection: self.mCollection];
    [myPlayer play];
}
```

To allow the Play button to work as a Play/Pause toggle, we can test the playBackState property of the music controller to see whether the music is playing or not and adjust the playback state accordingly. Because we have registered for playbackStateChanged: notifications, there's no need to make any changes to the playback button image; this is taken care of by the code handling the notification.

InfinitePlayback/PRPMusicViewController.m

```
- (IBAction)playButton:(UIButton *)sender {
    if (myPlayer.playbackState == MPMoviePlaybackStatePlaying) {
        [myPlayer pause];
    } else {
        [myPlayer play];
    }
}
```

When a notification is triggered, it calls the method we selected. The playingItemChanged: call allows us to update the track information in the display. We can use the nowPlayingItem method to fetch the data for the currently playing track and use the valueForProperty: method of the MPMediaItem class to retrieve text for each item that we need. We can also check to see whether the playBackState has changed and adjust the displayed text accordingly.

InfinitePlayback/PRPMusicViewController.m
```
- (void)playingItemChanged: (id) notification {
    MPMediaItem *currentItem = [myPlayer nowPlayingItem];
    albumName.text = [currentItem valueForProperty:
                                        MPMediaItemPropertyAlbumTitle];
    trackName.text = [currentItem valueForProperty:
                                        MPMediaItemPropertyTitle];
    if (myPlayer.playbackState == MPMusicPlaybackStateStopped) {
        trackName.text = @"PlayBack Complete";
    }
}
```

By responding to the state changes, we can set the image on the Play button to match the correct action—for example, Play when paused, and Pause when playing.

InfinitePlayback/PRPMusicViewController.m
```
- (void)playbackStateChanged: (id) notification {
    MPMusicPlaybackState playerState = [myPlayer playbackState];

    if (playerState == MPMusicPlaybackStatePaused) {
        [playPauseButton setImage:[UIImage imageNamed:
                                    @"mediumPlayButton.png"]
                                    forState:UIControlStateNormal];
    } else if (playerState == MPMusicPlaybackStatePlaying) {
        [playPauseButton setImage:[UIImage imageNamed:
                                    @"mediumPauseButton.png"]
                                    forState:UIControlStateNormal];
    } else if (playerState == MPMusicPlaybackStateStopped) {
        [playPauseButton setImage:[UIImage imageNamed:
                                    @"mediumPlayButton.png"]
                                    forState:UIControlStateNormal];
        [myPlayer stop];
    }
}
```

To draw the attention of the user to the newly available control, it's helpful to provide a little animation when we add the control to the view. The effect we use here is to "pop" the view onto the screen by using a scale transformation that gives the impression of the control zooming out toward us. When the music control is dismissed, we use the reverse effect, reducing the scale of the view to zero, so that the control zooms away from us. We do not need to specify a duration for the animation because the default value of 0.25 works nicely in this case. We only need to set the delegate for the ZoomOutView method because, in that case, we need to remove the view from its SuperView once the animation is complete.

InfinitePlayback/PRPMusicViewController.m
```
- (void)ZoomInView {

    self.view.layer.transform = CATransform3DMakeScale(1, 1, 1);
    CABasicAnimation *anim = [CABasicAnimation animation];
    anim.keyPath = @"transform.scale";
    anim.fromValue = [NSNumber numberWithFloat:0];
    anim.toValue = [NSNumber numberWithFloat:1.0];
    [self.view.layer addAnimation:anim forKey:@"scaleIn"];
}

- (void)ZoomOutView {

    CABasicAnimation *anim = [CABasicAnimation animation];
    anim.keyPath = @"transform.scale";
    anim.fromValue = [NSNumber numberWithFloat:1.0];
    anim.toValue = [NSNumber numberWithFloat:0];
    anim.removedOnCompletion = NO;
    anim.fillMode = kCAFillModeBoth;
    anim.delegate = self;
    [self.view.layer addAnimation:anim forKey:@"scaleOut"];
}

- (void)animationDidStop:(CABasicAnimation *)anim finished:(BOOL)flag {

    [self.view.layer removeAllAnimations];
    [self.view removeFromSuperview];
}
```

Now you have a reasonably functional album track player. You could still enhance the functionality by adding more controls, displaying more of the track metadata, allowing the option to scan ahead or backward in a track, or using a slider to control track playback position. All of those features follow the same general pattern established here and would not be too difficult for you to implement.

Recipe 13

Have Fun with Autoscrolling Text Views

Problem

Trying to make help screens or any other text view interesting can be a challenge. You want to add a little something to give your app a touch of style or to demonstrate that you, the developer, don't necessarily take yourself too seriously.

Solution

The sample app for this recipe, scrollingCredits, will make you either smile or grimace (see Figure 17, *Star-themed scrolling credits*, on page 63). Though it's meant to be quite lighthearted, this example contains some useful techniques. The three elements that are worth discussing in detail are using a transform for distorting the text, using Core Animation to make the text view autoscroll, and using the AVAudio framework to play back some music.

Working with 3D transforms can be a little challenging, but in general we create the matrices that produce the transformations using the library of methods that are defined for us by Core Animation, for example, scale (CATransform3DMakeScale), rotate (CATransform3DMakeRotation), and translate (CATransform3DMakeTranslation). We can also directly access the individual elements of the matrices to create some really interesting effects.

In the following code, you can see that Core Animation uses the CATransform3D type to hold the matrix; initially, we set this to CATransform3DIdentity, which is effectively an empty matrix. We can then directly access the individual elements by referring to the element number—in this case, m24—which controls the perspective scaling of the layer. We need to use relatively small numbers here, because large numbers will create so much perspective distortion that the majority of the layer will be offscreen. Here we simply want enough distortion to give the classic vanishing point-style effect.

ScrollingCredits/Classes/PRPScrollingTextViewController.m
```
CATransform3D trans = CATransform3DIdentity;
trans.m24 = -0.005;
```

Figure 17—Star-themed scrolling credits

We now have the transformation matrix, but we haven't actually applied it to anything, so we need to set up the text view that we will use for our rolling credits. The majority of this code is fairly straightforward and involves setting the properties for how we want the text view to appear, for example the font and color. We disable scrolling and editing because we do not need any user input. We also apply our transform matrix to the text view's layer to add the perspective effect.

The most unusual part of the text view setup is that we set the contentOffset to a large negative value for the y-axis. The result is that the text is set to be well below the view but ready to scroll up the screen as the animation starts. We set the animated property to NO because we will control the scrolling manually in the viewDidAppear: method.

ScrollingCredits/Classes/PRPScrollingTextViewController.m

```
CGFloat size = self.view.frame.size.height;
if (size > self.view.frame.size.width) size = self.view.frame.size.width;
CGRect frame = CGRectMake(self.view.frame.size.width/2 - size/4,
                                                  size/4,
                                                  size/2,
                                                  size/4*3);
textView = [[UITextView alloc] initWithFrame:frame];
self.textView.editable = NO;
self.textView.scrollEnabled = NO;
self.textView.font = [UIFont boldSystemFontOfSize:20];
self.textView.textAlignment = UITextAlignmentCenter;
self.textView.backgroundColor = [UIColor blackColor];
self.textView.textColor = [UIColor yellowColor];
self.textView.text = self.scrollText;
[self.view addSubview:self.textView];

self.textView.layer.transform = trans;
[self.textView setContentOffset:CGPointMake(0, -240) animated:NO];
```

We are using the viewDidAppear: method to trigger the animation because this ensures that the animation does not start until the view is visible to the user. Because we are animating a view property, contentOffset, we can use UIView animation to scroll the text. Using the Block style of animation, which was introduced in iOS 4.0, we specify the duration directly and the UIViewAnimationOptionCurveLinear animation curve as our only option. We set the final contentOffset position we want in the animations block; this animates the text to the top of the text view. There is no easy way to calculate the correct duration of the animation to coordinate with the length of the text we want to display, so we need to rely on a little experimentation to come up with a suitable value.

ScrollingCredits/Classes/PRPScrollingTextViewController.m

```
[UIView animateWithDuration:35 delay:0
                   options:UIViewAnimationOptionCurveLinear
                animations:^{[self.textView
                             setContentOffset:CGPointMake(0, 500)
                             animated:NO];}
                completion:NULL];
```

The humorous effect that the scrolling view adds would be lost without music to accompany it. Thankfully, the setup for playing a single piece of audio is quite simple. We need to establish the path to the compressed audio file so that we can create an instance of the AVAudioPLayer class that uses it. We set the numberOfLoops to 1, which prompts the audio to play twice, and we set the player to play. We could do a lot more with the AV audio player, but to keep this example simple, we're using the minimum amount of code we need to play the music.

ScrollingCredits/Classes/PRPScrollingTextViewController.m
```
NSURL *url = [NSURL fileURLWithPath:
                      [NSString stringWithFormat:@"%@/HeliumWars.m4a",
                      [[NSBundle mainBundle] resourcePath]]];

NSError *error;
audioPlayer = [[AVAudioPlayer alloc]
               initWithContentsOfURL:url error:&error];
audioPlayer.numberOfLoops = 1;
[audioPlayer play];
```

You now have a way of adding a small slice of whimsy to some of the more mundane sections of your app. You have some flexibility in how you display the text on the page—you can change the text, the music, and the scroll speed.

Recipe 14

Create a Custom Number Control

Problem

You need a way to let your user select a numeric value—perhaps the difficulty level or number of players in a game. You could use one of the UI components Apple provides, but its style might not fit the look and feel of the rest of your app.

Solution

We can solve this problem in a number of ways, but our best bet is to create a custom control that maximizes the use of the touch interface (see Figure 18, *The custom number spin control*, on page 67). Through table views we've become accustomed to the dynamic feedback of our actions, with the momentum-based scrolling letting us "flick" our way through a whole set of data. We could go with UIPickerView, but it has a very specific style and only a few options for customization. What we're looking for is something with similar mechanics but smaller in scope and more easily tailored to fit a particular UI style.

SWIZZLE, the free puzzle game in the App Store, uses just such a control as a means of selecting the game's difficulty level. Let's use an updated version of the code from that app, the SpinNumbers class, to walk through the technique for creating this style of control.

Like most of the UIKit control classes, such as buttons and sliders, SpinNumbers is a subclass of UIControl, which provides the methods we need to implement the target/action mechanism. This is the process by which the controller code can specify a selector to be called for a given event. Using the sendActionsForControlEvents: method, we can indirectly activate an action simply by specifying the appropriate control event. The UIControl base class code calls any selectors associated with that given event, so we don't need to worry about which events, if any, have actions defined.

Looking at our implementation, the primary task of the setup method is to create the visual components of the control. These elements are based entirely on transformed layers. We start by constructing a composite image of

Figure 18—The custom number spin control

the background and the label and then add the result as the content of each of the layers in turn. We apply an incrementing rotation transformation and positional translation to each layer, effectively adding it at the next position in a circle of layers.

To picture how this circle is constructed, imagine a playing card standing upright and a penny about 4 inches behind it. The card is our layer, and the penny is the center point of the circle we will create. Add another card next to the first, edges touching, and rotate it a little so that it is perpendicular to the penny. Repeat this until the cards form a complete circle around the penny.

As we construct our circle, each layer is added to a base layer, transformed, with a specific zPosition, equivalent to the radius of the circle, placing it at the correct distance from the center of the base layer. When we later rotate the base layer with a sublayer transform, the entire set of layers rotates as a single unit.

Say we want the control to have more of a three-dimensional appearance; we just add two semitransparent layers on top of the circle and to either side of the central layer. To give the impression of depth to the edges of the circle, we use gradients, from opaque to transparent, for the layer images—making it appear as though the center is spotlighted.

NumberSpinControl/NumberSpinControl/SpinNumbers.m

```objc
- (void)setup
{
    CGFloat width = self.bounds.size.width;
    self.cubeSize = self.bounds.size.height;
    self.tileRect = CGRectMake(0, 0, self.cubeSize, self.cubeSize);
    self.transformed = [CALayer layer];
    self.transformed.frame = self.bounds;
    self.transformed.backgroundColor = [UIColor blackColor].CGColor;
    [self.layer addSublayer:self.transformed];

    CATransform3D t = CATransform3DMakeTranslation((width-self.cubeSize)/2, 0, 0);

    for (int i =STARTNUM; i <= NUM ; i++) {
        self.label.text = [NSString stringWithFormat:@"%d",i];
        [self.transformed addSublayer:[self makeSurface:t]];
        t = CATransform3DRotate(t, RADIANS(self.rotAngle), 0, 1, 0);
        t = CATransform3DTranslate(t, self.cubeSize, 0, 0);
    }
    self.currentAngle = 0;
    self.currentTileNum = 0;

    CALayer *leftFade = [CALayer layer];
    leftFade.frame = CGRectMake(0, 0, width/2-5, self.cubeSize);
    leftFade.contents = (id)[UIImage imageNamed:@"leftFade.png"].CGImage;
    leftFade.opacity = 0.5;
    [self.layer addSublayer:leftFade];

    CALayer *rightFade = [CALayer layer];
    rightFade.frame = CGRectMake(width/2+5, 0, width/2, self.cubeSize);
    rightFade.contents = (id)[UIImage imageNamed:@"rightFade.png"].CGImage;
    rightFade.opacity = 0.5;
    [self.layer addSublayer:rightFade];
}
```

The makeSurface method creates and composites the new layer and applies the specified transform. The method needs to calculate the zPosition, the radius of our circle, based on the number of sides and the size of the layer.

NumberSpinControl/NumberSpinControl/SpinNumbers.m

```objc
- (CALayer*)makeSurface:(CATransform3D)t
{
    self.rotAngle = CIRCLE/NUM;
    CALayer *imageLayer = [CALayer layer];
```

```
imageLayer.anchorPoint = CGPointMake(1, 1);
float factor = (cos(RADIANS(self.rotAngle/2))/sin(RADIANS(self.rotAngle/2)))/2;
imageLayer.zPosition = self.cubeSize*factor;
imageLayer.frame = self.tileRect;
imageLayer.transform = t;

imageLayer.contents = (id)[self.backImage PRPCompositeView].CGImage;

return imageLayer;
}
```

To set up the features of the numeral we need—such as font size, alignment, and color—the getter for the label property contains a lazy initializer. Now we just need to update the text value as each layer's content is composited.

NumberSpinControl/NumberSpinControl/SpinNumbers.m
```
- (UILabel *)label
{
    if (!label) {
        label = [[UILabel alloc] initWithFrame:self.tileRect];
        label.textAlignment = UITextAlignmentCenter;
        label.font = [UIFont systemFontOfSize:self.cubeSize/1.4];
        label.backgroundColor = [UIColor clearColor];
        label.textColor = [UIColor whiteColor];
        label.shadowColor = [UIColor blackColor];
    }
    return label;
}
```

The backImage property is implemented in a similar way as the label. Note that the background color must be opaque and match the color of the background view. If the background color is set to clearColor, the layers now in the background become partly visible, which is probably undesirable.

NumberSpinControl/NumberSpinControl/SpinNumbers.m
```
- (UIImageView *)backImage
{
    if (!backImage) {
        backImage = [[UIImageView alloc] initWithImage:
                        [UIImage imageNamed:@"redBackground.png"]];
        backImage.frame = self.tileRect;
        backImage.backgroundColor = [UIColor blackColor];
        [backImage addSubview:self.label];
    }
    return backImage;
}
```

The beginTrackingWithTouch:withEvent: method initializes the touch recognition process by storing the initial touch position, which it uses for later comparison to the next touch.

NumberSpinControl/NumberSpinControl/SpinNumbers.m

```
- (BOOL)beginTrackingWithTouch:(UITouch*)touch withEvent:(UIEvent*)event
{
    CGPoint location = [touch locationInView:self];
    self.flick = 0;
    self.previousXPosition = location.x;
    self.beganLocation = location.x;
    newAngle = self.currentAngle;

    [self sendActionsForControlEvents:UIControlEventTouchDown];
    return YES;
}
```

As the user manipulates the control, the continueTrackingWithTouch:withEvent: method is called continuously. For each horizontal touch movement, we calculate the effective change in angle of the circle of layers and apply that as a rotation to the transformed parent layer. It is this transformation, based on the movement of the touch point, that provides the visual feedback to the user. The flick property is calculated to be a measure of velocity between the current touch point and the previous one.

NumberSpinControl/NumberSpinControl/SpinNumbers.m

```
- (BOOL)continueTrackingWithTouch:(UITouch *)touch withEvent:(UIEvent *)event
{
    CGPoint location = [touch locationInView:self];
    NSTimeInterval time = [touch timestamp];

    CGFloat locationDiff = self.beganLocation - location.x;
    self.flick = (self.previousXPosition-location.x)/(time-self.prevousTimeStamp);
    self.previousXPosition = location.x;
    self.prevousTimeStamp = time;
    self.newAngle = self.currentAngle - locationDiff/300*160;
    if (self.newAngle >= CIRCLE) self.newAngle -= CIRCLE;
    else if (self.newAngle < 0) self.newAngle += CIRCLE;

    [CATransaction setDisableActions:YES];
    self.transformed.sublayerTransform =
            CATransform3DMakeRotation(RADIANS(newAngle), 0, 1, 0);
    return YES;
}
```

The endTrackingWithTouch:withEvent: method uses the flick value to calculate which of the layers is predicted to be in front at the final position of the control after an appropriate amount of momentum. The real "trick" to making it appear as if the control has momentum is to animate the rotation of the ring of layers to the predicted number, over a fixed duration. If the flick value is high, then the change in number is greater, and the result is a larger rotation over the fixed time, showing the apparent speed. The animation uses the default easeout timing function, which adds a natural deceleration effect to the rotation before it stops at the predicted number.

NumberSpinControl/NumberSpinControl/SpinNumbers.m

```
- (void)endTrackingWithTouch:(UITouch *)touch withEvent:(UIEvent *)event
{
    CGPoint location = [touch locationInView:self];
    CGFloat halfWidth = self.bounds.size.width/2;
    int newNum = 0;
    if (self.flick == 0)
    {
        if (location.x > halfWidth + self.cubeSize/2) newNum = -1;
        if (location.x < halfWidth - self.cubeSize/2) newNum = 1;
    } else {
        newNum = self.flick / ACCELERATIONFACTOR;
        if (newNum > 150) newNum = 150;
        if (newNum < -150) newNum = -150;
    }
    self.newAngle = self.newAngle-newNum;
    if (self.newAngle < 0) self.newAngle = CIRCLE+self.newAngle;
    int tileNum = self.rotAngle/2;
    tileNum += self.newAngle;
    tileNum = tileNum%CIRCLE;
    tileNum = tileNum/self.rotAngle;
    tileNum = abs(tileNum-NUM)%NUM;

    [self moveToNewNumber:tileNum];
}
```

The moveToNewNumber method is called after the final touch or by the controller code to animate the control to a new value. We set up the rotation of the circle of layers and call sendActionsForControlEvents: with the UIControlEventValueChanged event to trigger any associated actions for that event.

NumberSpinControl/NumberSpinControl/SpinNumbers.m

```
-(void)moveToNewNumber:(int)newNumber
{
    self.newAngle = CIRCLE-newNumber*self.rotAngle;
    [CATransaction setValue:[NSNumber numberWithFloat:.5]
                    forKey:kCATransactionAnimationDuration];
    self.transformed.sublayerTransform =
                CATransform3DMakeRotation(RADIANS(self.newAngle), 0, 1, 0);
    self.currentTileNum = newNumber;
    self.currentAngle = self.newAngle;
    [self sendActionsForControlEvents: UIControlEventValueChanged];
}
```

Accessing the currentNumber property triggers the calculation of the *real* value of the control based on the relative position of the front-facing layer and the STARTNUM.

NumberSpinControl/NumberSpinControl/SpinNumbers.m

```
- (int)currentNumber
{
    return self.currentTileNum+STARTNUM;
}
```

Now that the SpinNumbers class is complete, let's look at how we would use it. We can add an instance directly to the NumberSpinControlViewController XIB in Interface Builder by adding a base UIView, setting its size and position as required, and then specifying the SpinNumbers class as the custom class in the Identity inspector. By linking the view to an IBOutlet in the NumberSpinControlViewController.m, we can set up the target/action mechanism to call our preferred method, numberChanged, when UIControlEventValueChanged has been detected.

NumberSpinControl/NumberSpinControl/NumberSpinControlViewController.m

```
- (void)viewDidLoad
{
    [super viewDidLoad];
    [numbers addTarget:self action:@selector(numberChanged)
                        forControlEvents:UIControlEventValueChanged];
    [numbers moveToNewNumber:2];
}
```

We know that the UIControlEventValueChanged event is triggered only when we have detected an end to touches on the control and established the extent of the control rotation. We are able to access the derived value of the currentNumber property value and use that to update the label accordingly. It's worth noting that the value appears to change before the rotational momentum of the control has stopped. This is because it is triggered before the half-second animation that we use to imply the frictional slowdown of the spinning wheel. We could experiment a little here and alter the effect by triggering an additional event at the end of the momentum animation and using that to update the label.

NumberSpinControl/NumberSpinControl/NumberSpinControlViewController.m

```
- (void)numberChanged
{
    numLabel.text = [NSString stringWithFormat:@"%d", numbers.currentNumber];
}
```

Though complete in itself, the code we've worked through here really covers only the basic elements of a control; we could add many enhancements to make it more configurable. You could increase the number of external properties, color, and images, for example; allow for both vertical and horizontal presentation; or allow for different sequences, such as letters or symbols. The options are limited only by your imagination!

CHAPTER 2

Table and Scroll View Recipes

UIScrollView and its popular subclass UITableView are two powerful and versatile tools for iOS developers. They mask an incredible amount of complexity and save you the time and heartache of having to make a comparable solution yourself—exactly what any API should do.

As the iOS platform has matured, a number of patterns have emerged that have led to redundant work done in many (if not all) projects. The recipes in this section aim to identify and tackle those areas where things could be a little simpler. They're designed to save you time and effort while staying out of the way of whatever you're planning to do. Most of the traditional patterns laid out by UIKit are preserved in order to make these recipes easy for you to understand.

Recipe 15

Simplify Table Cell Production

Problem

UIKit provides an efficient reuse mechanism for table view cells, keeping overhead low and minimizing costly allocations that slow down scrolling. Although this mechanism works well to curb resource consumption, it tends to be verbose, repetitive, and, most of all, error prone. This common pattern begs for a solution that minimizes controller code and maximizes reuse across multiple views or even applications.

Solution

A basic UITableView layout, as seen in the iPod and Contacts applications, is simple enough to re-create without causing too many headaches: the cells all use the same boilerplate UITableViewCellStyle. Once we venture outside of this comfort zone, however, our code can get messy rather quickly. Consider a custom cell with two images and a text label. Our -tableView:cellForRowAtIndexPath: method may start off like this:

```
static NSString *CellID = @"CustomCell";

UITableViewCell *cell = [tableView
                   dequeueReusableCellWithIdentifier:CellID];
if (cell == nil) {
  cell = [[[UITableViewCell alloc]
              initWithStyle:UITableViewCellStyleDefault
            reuseIdentifier:CellID]
       autorelease];
  UIImage *rainbow = [UIImage imageNamed:@"rainbow.png"];
  UIImageView *mainImageView = [[UIImageView alloc] initWithImage:rainbow];
  UIImageView *otherImageView = [[UIImageView alloc] initWithImage:rainbow];
  CGRect iconFrame = (CGRect) { { 12.0, 4.0 }, rainbow.size };
  mainImageView.frame = iconFrame;
  iconFrame.origin.x = CGRectGetMaxX(iconFrame) + 9.0;
  altImageView.frame = iconFrame;

  [cell.contentView addSubview:mainImageView];
  [cell.contentView addSubview:otherImageView];
  UILabel *label = [[UILabel alloc] initWithFrame:labelFrame];
  [cell.contentView addSubview:label];
```

```
    [mainIcon release];
    [otherIcon release];
    [label release];
}

return cell;
```

Note we haven't even configured the cell yet! When reusing a cell, how do we get at those now-anonymous subviews that were added during creation? We have two options: set tag literals on the subviews, which we then use to fish them back out at reuse time; or write a UITableViewCell subclass with explicit properties. Going the subclass route is much more attractive because it does the following:

- Defines a contract (properties) for accessing the subviews

- Avoids the danger of tag collisions in the cell hierarchy (multiple subviews with the same tag)

- Decouples the cell's layout from the view controller, enabling code reuse across views and projects

By using a subclass, we get a number of other opportunities to simplify the table-building process. Every table view data source inevitably has the same cell dequeue/alloc code in it. This code is not just redundant; it's also fragile: a misspelled cell identifier, a single instead of a double equals in our nil check—subtle errors lead to performance hits and wasted debugging time. If we didn't have to constantly copy and paste this redundant code, or even look at it, our routine for building table views would be much less tedious.

Enter PRPSmartTableViewCell: a foundational subclass of UITableViewCell that eliminates clutter in our table view controllers and prevents costly bugs in our scattered cell boilerplate. The class's primary task is to abstract away that boilerplate so that, ideally, we never have to worry about it again. The class has a special initializer method and two convenience methods, which we'll explore next.

SmarterTableCells/Classes/PRPSmartTableViewCell.h

```
@interface PRPSmartTableViewCell : UITableViewCell {}

+ (id)cellForTableView:(UITableView *)tableView;
+ (NSString *)cellIdentifier;

- (id)initWithCellIdentifier:(NSString *)cellID;

@end
```

The +cellForTableView: class method handles cell reuse for a table view that's passed by the caller—our table view controller.

SmarterTableCells/Classes/PRPSmartTableViewCell.m
```
+ (id)cellForTableView:(UITableView *)tableView {
    NSString *cellID = [self cellIdentifier];
    UITableViewCell *cell = [tableView
                            dequeueReusableCellWithIdentifier:cellID];
    if (cell == nil) {
        cell = [[[self alloc] initWithCellIdentifier:cellID] autorelease];
    }
    return cell;
}
```

This code should look familiar: it's nearly identical to the reuse code you've surely written dozens (if not hundreds) of times as an iOS developer. Note, however, that the cell identifier string is obtained from another class method: +cellIdentifier. This method uses the cell's class name as the identifier by default, even for subclasses of PRPSmartTableViewCell you write. Now, whenever we decide to write a custom cell class, we're guaranteed a unique cell identifier for free. Note that the identifier is not marked static as you've seen in most sample code, so there is some extra allocation going on in the default implementation. If you find this to be a problem, you can always override (or edit) +cellIdentifier to change its behavior.

SmarterTableCells/Classes/PRPSmartTableViewCell.m
```
+ (NSString *)cellIdentifier {
    return NSStringFromClass([self class]);
}
```

Finally, we use a new designated initializer, -initWithCellIdentifier:, to set up the cell and its layout. This is where we'd put the verbose layout code that would otherwise live in our controller.

SmarterTableCells/Classes/PRPSmartTableViewCell.m
```
- (id)initWithCellIdentifier:(NSString *)cellID {
    return [self initWithStyle:UITableViewCellStyleSubtitle
            reuseIdentifier:cellID];
}
```

With this new pattern, here's how we'd write and use our table cell subclass:

1. Create a subclass of PRPSmartTableViewCell.

2. Override -initWithCellIdentifier:.

3. Call +cellForTableView: from our table view controller.

Now let's take a look at our table view controller code for producing a custom PRPSmartTableViewCell:

SmarterTableCells/Classes/PRPRainbowTableViewController.m
```
- (UITableViewCell *)tableView:(UITableView *)tableView
        cellForRowAtIndexPath:(NSIndexPath *)indexPath {
    PRPDoubleRainbowCell *cell = [PRPDoubleRainbowCell
                                  cellForTableView:tableView];
    cell.mainLabel.text = [self.quotes objectAtIndex:indexPath.row];
    return cell;
}
```

The controller code is significantly reduced and much more readable—it now contains only the customization of the cell for that particular view. All the cell's characteristic logic and layout is hidden away in the cell class, allowing it to be easily reused anywhere else in this or another project. If you were planning to write a UITableViewCell subclass, this additional code could save you a lot of work in the long run. If you're writing a basic table view with one of the standard cell types, it could be overkill.

This pattern pays especially large dividends when you're writing a heavily customized table view with assorted types of cells. We'll explore this further in Recipe 18, *Organize Complex Table Views*, on page 86.

You can also easily extend this pattern to use custom cells created in Interface Builder, as you'll see in the next recipe.

Recipe 16

Use Smart Table Cells in a Nib

Problem

The previous recipe, Recipe 15, *Simplify Table Cell Production*, on page 74, showed you how to create a complex custom table cell with ease while significantly reducing the amount of controller code you have to write. What if you prefer to create your cells in Interface Builder?

Solution

The "smart table cell" pattern we just explored is easily adaptable to nib-based cells. As is usually the case when using Interface Builder (IB), we end up saving even more code than before. We'll apply the same core principle of abstracting the reuse labor away from the controller, but the controller does need to contribute a little more than it did last time. Specifically, we'll ask the controller to manage the nib.

Our PRPNibBasedTableViewCell seems very familiar if you've reviewed PRPSmartTableViewCell: it has a +cellIdentifier method that returns a custom reuse identifier, and it has a convenience method for the typical dequeue-or-instantiate dance we do for every table cell we create.

SmarterTableCellsNib/Shared/PRPNibBasedTableViewCell.m
```
+ (NSString *)cellIdentifier {
    return NSStringFromClass([self class]);
}
```

SmarterTableCellsNib/Shared/PRPNibBasedTableViewCell.m
```
+ (id)cellForTableView:(UITableView *)tableView fromNib:(UINib *)nib {
    NSString *cellID = [self cellIdentifier];
    UITableViewCell *cell = [tableView
                          dequeueReusableCellWithIdentifier:cellID];
    if (cell == nil) {
        NSArray *nibObjects = [nib instantiateWithOwner:nil options:nil];

        NSAssert2(([nibObjects count] > 0) &&
                  [[nibObjects objectAtIndex:0] isKindOfClass:[self class]],
                  @"Nib '%@' does not appear to contain a valid %@",
                  [self nibName], NSStringFromClass([self class]));
```

```
        cell = [nibObjects objectAtIndex:0];
    }
    return cell;
}
```

Note the generation method is a little different here: it takes a second parameter for a UINib object. UINib is a new class designed to minimize overhead when rapidly instantiating views from a nib file. Rather than calling -[NSBundle loadNibNamed:owner:options:], we hold onto our UINib object and call -instantiateWithOwner:options: to get a fresh copy of our nib objects.

In this recipe, we ask the calling code—presumably a UITableViewDataSource—to hold onto that nib, but we still make it easy as possible to get one. The +nib and +nibName methods provide easy access to the nib that hosts our custom cell.

SmarterTableCellsNib/Shared/PRPNibBasedTableViewCell.m

```
+ (UINib *)nib {
    NSBundle *classBundle = [NSBundle bundleForClass:[self class]];
    return [UINib nibWithNibName:[self nibName] bundle:classBundle];
}

+ (NSString *)nibName {
    return [self cellIdentifier];
}
```

The methods are straightforward enough: +nib looks in the class's bundle, using the name returned by +nibName. By default, +nibName relies on +cellIdentifier, which defaults to the classname. This default behavior should scale to any number of subclasses, as long as we configure our files accordingly.

Let's take a look at this pattern in practice. Open the SmarterTableCellsNib project and navigate to the PRPComplexTableViewCell class. This class inherits from the PRPNibBasedTableViewCell class. Note that there's hardly any code—just properties representing some of the cell's subviews, which are in the nib. PRPComplexTableViewCell has a few important characteristics that make it work:

- It subclasses PRPNibBasedTableViewCell.

- Its XIB filename matches the class name (PRPComplexTableViewCell.xib).

- Its cell identifier matches the class name (PRPComplexTableViewCell).

- The table cell is the first object in the nib.

That last part is important. Taking a closer look at the implementation of +cellForTableView:fromNib:, we note that it throws an explanatory error if our nib contains something other than an instance of our cell subclass at the top.

Set Your Nib's Cell Identifier!

Whether or not you use this recipe, remember to set the Identifier attribute for every table view cell you create in Interface Builder. (See Figure 19, *Reuse identifiers in Interface Builder*, on page 81.) This is a common oversight when using Interface Builder to create a table cell; you may fool yourself into thinking you've done it when you write the standard reuse code. You haven't!

This careless mistake has huge performance implications. Always check your work by either setting a breakpoint or adding a log statement to your cell creation logic. You shouldn't be instantiating any new cell objects after the initial burst when the table view is shown. If you're instantiating cells indefinitely, the identifier set in your nib most likely does not match the identifier you're using to produce the cell.

We name the files and attributes accordingly to match the behavior inherited from PRPNibBasedTableViewCell. If we write our own subclass with a name that does not match the accompanying xib filename and/or cell identifier, no problem: we just override +cellIdentifier and +nibName in the subclass to return the appropriate strings.

As explained earlier, the calling code holds onto the generated nib. The SmarterTableCellsNib project includes a TestViewController class demonstrating how to do this.

1. Declare a property for the nib.

2. Create a lazy initializer to make the nib available on demand for any use case.

3. Clean up the property in -viewDidUnload and -dealloc.

SmarterTableCellsNib/Shared/TestViewController.h
```
@interface TestViewController : UITableViewController {}

@property (nonatomic, retain) UINib *complexCellNib;

@end
```

SmarterTableCellsNib/Shared/TestViewController.m
```
- (UINib *)complexCellNib {
    if (complexCellNib == nil) {
        self.complexCellNib = [PRPComplexTableViewCell nib];
    }
    return complexCellNib;
}
```

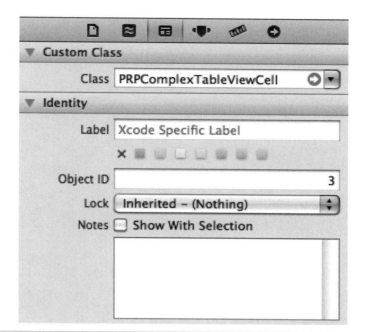

Figure 19—Reuse identifiers in Interface Builder

SmarterTableCellsNib/Shared/TestViewController.m
```
- (void)viewDidUnload {
    [super viewDidUnload];
    self.complexCellNib = nil;
}

- (void)dealloc {
    [complexCellNib release], complexCellNib = nil;
    [super dealloc];
}
```

Once we have a valid nib, we pass it to +cellForTableView:fromNib: from our -tableView:cellForRowAtIndexPath: method. The default implementation takes it from there.

SmarterTableCellsNib/Shared/TestViewController.m
```
- (UITableViewCell *)tableView:(UITableView *)tableView
        cellForRowAtIndexPath:(NSIndexPath *)indexPath {
    PRPComplexTableViewCell *cell =
        [PRPComplexTableViewCell cellForTableView:tableView
                                    fromNib:self.complexCellNib];

    cell.titleLabel.text = [NSString stringWithFormat:@"Cell #%d",
                            indexPath.row];
```

```
cell.dateLabel.text =
    [NSDateFormatter localizedStringFromDate:[NSDate date]
                                   dateStyle:NSDateFormatterNoStyle
                                   timeStyle:NSDateFormatterMediumStyle];
cell.locationLabel.text = @"Places unknown";

return cell;
}
```

And we're done. With this recipe in place, you have two highly reusable techniques for rapid, clean use of custom table cells.

Recipe 17

Locate Table Cell Subviews

Problem

We all inevitably work on projects that require custom table view cell layouts. If these cells include controls or buttons, figuring out which row contains a given button can be difficult. How can you find an arbitrary button's parent cell in a way that works for any layout or project?

Solution

Finding the row that hosts a custom view or control is not particularly hard. The problem is, it's easy to do wrong.

Let's say each of our table cells has a button that uses our table view controller as a target. When the user taps any one of these buttons, the same single action is called. What if our table has 100 rows? We need to distinguish one row from another to know which button or row the user tapped.

```
- (IBAction)cellButtonTapped:(id)sender {
        // Which table row is this button in?
}
```

Figure 20, *What's the index path for a given button?*, on page 84 illustrates the problem at hand. There's no easy or obvious way for your code to tell one cell button from another.

The tempting course of action would be to just walk right up the tree to the hosting table cell and ask the table view which row that cell corresponds to. After all, we know our own cell's hierarchy.

```
- (IBAction)cellButtonTapped:(id)sender {
        // Go get the enclosing cell manually
        UITableViewCell *parentCell = [[sender superview] superview];
        NSIndexPath *pathForButton = [self.tableView
                indexPathForCell:parentCell];
}
```

This approach is probably the quickest, but it's far from ideal, for a few reasons. First, it's fragile. The previous code assumes the cell hierarchy won't change. But if we move this button up or down one level, this code

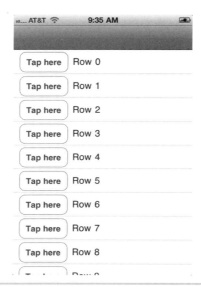

Figure 20—What's the index path for a given button?

immediately breaks—and we may not remember why, or even notice, until the worst possible moment. Walking up the tree iteratively until we find a UITableViewCell is not a whole lot better. We want something short, sweet, and minimally error-prone.

Second, the previous solutions aren't portable. The work we do here is likely to be done again for our next fancy interactive table. It would be great to have a solution we could drop into any project.

Let's start by talking about a cleaner way to find the view's enclosing row. UIView has some handy methods that allow us to translate points on the screen from one view's coordinates to another's. We can use this -convertPoint:toView: method to figure out where in our table view the tapped button resides; we'll bypass the cell entirely. Once we have that adjusted point, we'll pass it to -[UITableView indexPathForRowAtPoint:] and get our row index.

CellSubviewLocation/Classes/RootViewController.m
```
- (IBAction)cellButtonTapped:(id)sender {
    UIButton *button = sender;
    CGPoint correctedPoint =
      [button convertPoint:button.bounds.origin toView:self.tableView];
    NSIndexPath *indexPath =
      [self.tableView indexPathForRowAtPoint:correctedPoint];
    NSLog(@"Button tapped in row %d", indexPath.row);
}
```

This doesn't involve any more code than the earlier "lazy" approaches, and it's safer and more portable. We can make it even more portable if we want. Those two lines of code are hardly difficult to move around, but the convertPoint: methods are subtle enough that revisiting them months later can lead to some head-scratching. It'd be nice to solve this problem once and get back to business.

To do that, we'll place this logic in a UITableView category. We'll have to make some adjustments because the work is now being done by the table view instead of the table view controller, but the idea is the same.

CellSubviewLocation/Classes/UITableView+PRPSubviewAdditions.m

```
@implementation UITableView (PRPSubviewAdditions)

- (NSIndexPath *)prp_indexPathForRowContainingView:(UIView *)view {
    CGPoint correctedPoint = [view convertPoint:view.bounds.origin
                                         toView:self];
    return [self indexPathForRowAtPoint:correctedPoint];
}

@end
```

Now that we've abstracted the busywork of converting the point to an index path, our table view controller just passes the relevant view and gets back the source index path.

```
- (IBAction)cellButtonTapped:(id)sender {
    NSIndexPath *pathForButton =
        [self.tableView prp_indexPathForRowContainingView:sender];
}
```

This recipe gives us a clean solution to tracing the origin of embedded table cell controls, no matter how the table or the cell is laid out.

Recipe 18

Organize Complex Table Views

Credit

This recipe was inspired in no small part by Fraser Speirs' excellent article, "A technique for using UITableView and retaining your sanity," at speirs.org.

Problem

Working with UITableView is easy when you have a uniform dataset. Once you need to do something special in a particular section or row, however, things can get out of hand quickly. How can you cleanly build a table view with diverse rows, like the one seen in the Settings application?

Solution

This kind of problem can sneak up on us. Let's say we have some in-app settings to manage or a few high-level navigation options that are always present. We start with a simple table with identical rows for each of the choices. Easy enough: create an array for the intended titles and use that to build the table's rows.

```
-(void)viewDidLoad {
        self.rowTitles = [NSArray arrayWithObjects:@"Favorite Team",
                                        @"Favorite Color",
                                        @"Alerts", nil];
}
- (NSInteger)numberOfSectionsInTableView:(UITableView)tableView {
        return 1;
}
- (NSInteger)tableView:(UITableView)tableView
            numberOfRowsInSection:(NSInteger)section {
        return [self.rowTitles count];
}
```

Looks good, right? We use the array to determine the number of rows and now just index the array in -tableView:cellForRowAtIndexPath: to get our cell titles.

```
cell.textLabel.text = [self.rowTitles objectAtIndex:indexPath.row];
```

So, each of these cells, when tapped, performs a completely different task. It's not like Contacts, where we just present the person detail screen with the selected data. Each row will push its own unique detail interface. Now things get complicated, starting with -tableView:didSelectCellForRowAtIndexPath:.

```
switch (indexPath.row) {
        case 0:
                // Push the team selection view controller
                break;
        case 1:
                // Push the color selection view controller
                break;
        case 2:
                // Push the alerts view controller
                break;
        default:
                NSLog(@"GAME OVER, MAN! GAME OVER!");
                break;
}
```

The use of magic numbers here is an immediate red flag. We could declare constants to use here instead, but that's really just masking the problem: our logic for creating the rows (a switch statement tied to literals) has been decoupled from our logic for setting them up (the array).

Let's make things more complicated. Our designer tells us the alerts row should have a different appearance. Now we need to add a similar switch statement blob to -tableView:cellForRowAtIndexPath:, which until now was relatively clean. We may even be looking at multiple reuse identifiers to represent the new cell layouts.

It gets worse. We've decided that "favorite color" should come before "favorite team" in the list. Now we have to reorder your array and shuffle around every piece of code that checks the row index. Right now, that's just cell creation and selection. What if we decide to customize the cell height? The background color? What if we have a table where some cells are editable and others aren't? Each of these scenarios yields yet another data source or delegate method relying on this fragile technique. If we forget to change one area or type the wrong number, we end up with misplaced behavior or even exceptions because of an out-of-bounds index.

Actually, scratch that: alerts should be in a different section. Now we need a two-dimensional switch statement—one for sections, one for rows—and a two-dimensional array for all the row titles. If we forget to increase the hard-coded number of sections, data will disappear. If we later reduce the

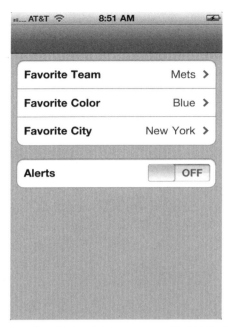

Unstructured data can be difficult to manage with UITableView. Note how each row in the first section is unique, and each section has an explicit number and order of rows.

Figure 21—Heterogeneous table view layout

number of sections, we have exposed ourselves to another out-of-bounds exception from stale indexing logic.

How did it come to this? Everything was so simple at first. The (allegedly) final design can be seen in Figure 21, *Heterogeneous table view layout*, on page 88.

Your interface doesn't always line up with a basic data structure where each row is bound to an item in an array. Forcing the issue won't change anything: we're developing a specialized view, so we need a specialized solution.

The only real value of the array in this example is to give us an abstracted row count. We can get that, as well as readable, flexible row indexes, by using enumerations. We start by enumerating all the sections we want. The first element is initialized to zero, which is the first valid section and row index in a table view.

OrganizedTableView/Classes/RootViewController.m

```
enum PRPTableSections {
    PRPTableSectionFavorites = 0,
    PRPTableSectionAlerts,
    PRPTableNumSections,
};
```

Note that the final PRPTableNumSections value is not a section identifier. It's a natural count of the sections in our table view, since it follows the last section. This is very convenient for -numberOfSectionsInTableView:.

OrganizedTableView/Classes/RootViewController.m

```
- (NSInteger)numberOfSectionsInTableView:(UITableView *)tableView {
    return PRPTableNumSections;
}
```

We do the same for our table rows, declaring a separate enum for each section to ensure the indexes will be right. The system immediately begins to pay off when returning the number of rows in each section: we've eliminated the magic numbers and also made the code more readable for future maintenance.

OrganizedTableView/Classes/RootViewController.m

```
enum PRPFavoritesRows {
    PRPTableSecFavoritesRowTeam = 0,
    PRPTableSecFavoritesRowColor,
    PRPTableSecFavoritesRowCity,
    PRPTableSecFavoritesNumRows,
};
enum PRPAlertsRows {
    PRPTableSecAlertsRowAlerts = 0,
    PRPTableSecAlertsNumRows,
};
```

OrganizedTableView/Classes/RootViewController.m

```
switch (section) {
    case PRPTableSectionFavorites:
        return PRPTableSecFavoritesNumRows;
    case PRPTableSectionAlerts:
        return PRPTableSecAlertsNumRows;
    default:
        NSLog(@"Unexpected section (%d)", section);
        break;
}
```

The -tableView:cellForRowAtIndexPath: method combines the enums and produces the appropriate content. It starts by checking the requested section against the PRPTableSections enum and then the row against the corresponding row enum for that section.

OrganizedTableView/Classes/RootViewController.m
```
switch (indexPath.section) {
    case PRPTableSectionFavorites:
        cell = [PRPBasicSettingsCell cellForTableView:tableView];
        switch (indexPath.row) {
            case PRPTableSecFavoritesRowTeam:
                cell.textLabel.text = @"Favorite Team";
                cell.detailTextLabel.text = @"Mets";
                break;
            case PRPTableSecFavoritesRowColor:
                cell.textLabel.text = @"Favorite Color";
                cell.detailTextLabel.text = @"Blue";
                break;
            case PRPTableSecFavoritesRowCity:
                cell.textLabel.text = @"Favorite City";
                cell.detailTextLabel.text = @"New York";
                break;
            default:
                NSAssert1(NO, @"Unexpected row in Favorites section: %d",
                          indexPath.row);
                break;
        }
        break;
```

OrganizedTableView/Classes/RootViewController.m
```
case PRPTableSectionAlerts:
    switch (indexPath.row) {
        case PRPTableSecAlertsRowAlerts: {
            PRPSwitchSettingsCell *alertCell =
                [PRPSwitchSettingsCell cellForTableView:tableView];
            alertCell.textLabel.text = @"Alerts";
            alertCell.cellSwitch.on = NO;
            cell = alertCell;
        }
            break;
        default:
            NSAssert1(NO, @"Unexpected row in Alerts section: %d",
                      indexPath.row);
            break;
    }
    break;
default:
    NSAssert1(NO, @"Unexpected section (%d)", indexPath.section);
    break;
```

So, our table has a structured, predictable, readable flow. Now let's talk about those pesky design changes. Our Favorites section has three rows: Favorite Team, Color, and City. You decide that City should come before Color, not after. To solve this problem *for the entire class*, you just rearrange the enum.

Generating Static Table Cells

The OrganizedTableView project accompanying this recipe uses subclasses to obscure the standard table cell reuse mechanism. If your table view has a small number of cells, it may be more appropriate to simply store each individual cell in properties and avoid table cell reuse altogether. Review "The Technique for Static Row Content" in Apple's Table View Programming Guide for iOS document before deciding how to store and generate your table cells.

```
enum PRPFavoritesRows {
    PRPTableSecFavoritesRowTeam = 0,
    PRPTableSecFavoritesRowCity,
    PRPTableSecFavoritesRowColor,
    PRPTableSecFavoritesNumRows,
};
```

Every piece of code in this class checks against the enum declaration, so now City comes before Color in all our rows, and all the behavior—cell creation, selection, height, background, editing style—still matches up. The beautiful thing is that we didn't need to touch or even look at any of it.

What if you want to remove the City row altogether? Easy: move it to the end of the enum, below PRPTableSecFavoritesNumRows, or just comment it out. We have simultaneously removed the City row from the usable list and decreased the total number of rows, with no other code changes. All the logic to create and handle the City row are still there, but it will just never be hit. It's hard to believe, but try it. We've now made a risk-free change to our design that we can change right back in seconds. No more copies, pastes, undos, or source control reverts.

There's something else going on here. The project uses multiple cell styles; where are the cell identifiers? The -dequeueReusableCellWithIdentifier: messages? They're hidden away in PRPSmartTableViewCell subclasses, building on the earlier Recipe 15, *Simplify Table Cell Production*, on page 74. Think about how much more code there would be without employing this additional technique, especially as the table's complexity increases.

With this recipe, we've shown you a technique for writing a complex table view in a way that won't make your head spin when you come back to it six months later. We hope it will also reduce the amount of work you need to do when it's time to change things up.

Recipe 19

Produce Two-Tone Table Views

Problem

You like the two-tone appearance of the App Store and other apps, but UITableView lets you set only a single background color. How do you produce a smooth, easy table with different colors for the top and bottom?

Solution

UITableView offers an incredible amount of customization through its data source and delegate protocol methods, its header and footer views, and the versatile UITableViewCell. None of these options, however, gets us a table with different "background" colors on each end. To do this, we'll write a clever UITableView subclass that's also easy to reuse and customize. Figure 22, *Two-tone table view layout*, on page 93 illustrates the effect this recipe produces.

Let's look at the problem first. We can set the backgroundColor property on a table view easily enough, which colors the empty space that appears while scrolling beyond the table's bounds. However, backgroundColor also affects the color of the table cells by default, so that's not an ideal solution. We can view this effect by running the TwoToneTables project and tapping the Custom Background row.

So, how do we make the top a slightly different color from the rest of the table? That's easy: we just set a table header. We can do this using a special PRPGradientView class that exposes the handy capabilities of CAGradientLayer. Now our header makes a smooth transition from the main background color to a slightly darker color up top.

TwoToneTables/Classes/DemoTableViewController.m

```
- (void)installHeader {
    CGRect headerFrame = CGRectMake(0, 0, self.tableView.frame.size.width,
                                    50.0);
    PRPGradientView *header = [[PRPGradientView alloc]
                               initWithFrame:headerFrame];
    [header setGradientColors:[NSArray arrayWithObjects:
                               (id)[self altBackgroundColor].CGColor,
                               (id)self.tableView.backgroundColor.CGColor,
                               nil]];
```

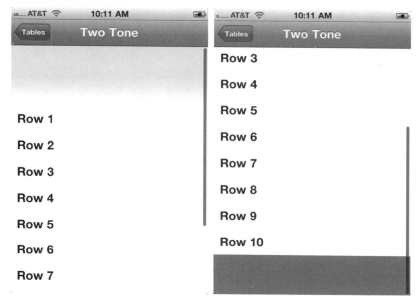

The solution we're seeking displays different colors at either end of the table, as illustrated in these two screenshots. The table has a white gradient on top and a red background on the bottom. A traditional table view displays only a single background color beyond the top and bottom content edges.

(Please don't ship an app with clashing colors like this. We're only using them here to make the contrast obvious.)

Figure 22—Two-tone table view layout

```
    self.tableView.tableHeaderView = header;
    header.backgroundColor = [self demoBackgroundColor];
    [header release];
}
```

This looks great—until we pull down on the table. That smooth gradient ends abruptly, and the lighter table background reappears above it. How do we make that darker color persist at the top while keeping the lighter color everywhere else? A table footer view won't help for the same reason a header didn't. We need to get a little more creative than that.

A UITableView subclass called PRPTwoToneTableView solves this problem. It declares topColor and bottomColor properties to be set by the caller—our view controller, for example. Using these top and bottom properties, plus the backgroundColor property, we can even make a three-tone table view if we want.

```
TwoToneTables/Classes/PRPTwoToneTableView.h
@interface PRPTwoToneTableView : UITableView {}


@property (nonatomic, retain) UIColor *topColor;
@property (nonatomic, retain) UIColor *bottomColor;


@end
```

These "colors" are really two "stretcher" subviews that our table adds auto-matically. These views let us customize the edge colors while still using our own table header and footer views. Note that we're still using the gradient view for a table header just as we were before. We declare them as properties in a private class extension and tie them to the public color properties in custom setter methods.

```
TwoToneTables/Classes/PRPTwoToneTableView.m
@interface PRPTwoToneTableView ()


@property (nonatomic, retain) UIView *topStretcher;
@property (nonatomic, retain) UIView *bottomStretcher;


@end
```

```
TwoToneTables/Classes/PRPTwoToneTableView.m
- (void)setTopColor:(UIColor *)color {
    if (self.topStretcher == nil) {
        topStretcher = [[UIView alloc] initWithFrame:CGRectZero];
        [self addSubview:self.topStretcher];
    }

    if (self.topStretcher.backgroundColor != color) {
        self.topStretcher.backgroundColor = color;
    }
}
```

How do these new subviews solve the problem? How do they not interfere with normal table view behavior? The answer lies in the -layoutSubviews method, which any UIView subclass can implement. UITableView already does a great deal of work in this method, and PRPTwoToneTableView simply builds on that.

Our custom -layoutSubviews method simulates a different "background" color on either end of the table by stretching the new subviews to fill the space left when scrolling past either end. We adjust the appropriate stretcher view according to the table's current contentOffset—think "scroll point"—and we're done. This works because each incremental scroll affects a scroll or table view's bounds, which produces a -layoutSubviews message for our table.

First things first: when overriding layoutSubviews on a class like UITableView, don't forget to call [super layoutSubviews] before doing your own work. If you prevent UITableView from performing its own layout operations, you won't have much of a table view: comment out the message to super in -[PRPTwoToneTableView layoutSubviews], and you'll notice that none of the cells appears.

When we pull down on a table that's already at the top, the table's contentOffset.y value becomes negative. We check for this when deciding to show and adjust our top stretcher to fill the gap. This produces the top "background" color.

TwoToneTables/Classes/PRPTwoToneTableView.m
```
- (void)layoutSubviews {
    [super layoutSubviews];
    if (self.topStretcher) {
        if (self.contentOffset.y > 0) {
            self.topStretcher.hidden = YES;
        } else {
            self.topStretcher.frame = CGRectMake(0, self.contentOffset.y,
                                                 self.frame.size.width,
                                                 -self.contentOffset.y);
            self.topStretcher.hidden = NO;
        }
    }
}
```

We handle the bottom stretcher in a similar fashion, but it's a little more complicated. The bottom of the view is not exactly a fixed value like the top is, so first we have to find out whether the bottom is on-screen. From there, we show the bottom stretcher if appropriate and adjust it to fill the gap.

TwoToneTables/Classes/PRPTwoToneTableView.m
```
CGFloat contentBottom = (self.contentSize.height - self.contentOffset.y);
CGFloat bottomGap = self.frame.size.height - contentBottom;
if ((bottomGap > 0) && self.bottomStretcher) {
    if (self.contentOffset.y < 0) {
        self.bottomStretcher.hidden = YES;
    } else {
        self.bottomStretcher.frame = CGRectMake(0, self.contentSize.height,
                                                self.frame.size.width,
                                                bottomGap);
        self.bottomStretcher.hidden = NO;
    }
} else {
    self.bottomStretcher.hidden = YES;
}
```

More often than not, we can accomplish a two-tone appearance by setting the standard background color, which extends to the bottom automatically, and then setting a custom topColor on our new subclass. We'd set bottomColor only if we wanted a three-tone table with different top, middle, and bottom colors.

We could do a good amount of this work in UIScrollViewDelegate methods on our table view controller, but we'd have to move that code around to every controller we wrote. By overriding -layoutSubviews in a subclass of UITableView, we've dramatically simplified the process of creating this two-tone effect. We don't need to remember to implement or connect anything in our controller code—we just create a PRPTwoToneTableView and set our colors, and we can be on our way.

In the next recipe, Recipe 20, *Add Border Shadows for Table Views*, on page 97, we take this technique to the next level by automatically adding drop shadows to the borders of a table view.

Recipe 20

Add Border Shadows for Table Views

Problem

You want to add some depth to your table views. How do you get an effect like the one you see in the Clock app, in a way that is both easy and reusable?

Solution

In a number of Apple apps, table views are decorated with border shadows to give some depth and character to their appearance. The most visible examples are the World Clock, Alarm, and Stopwatch tabs in the Clock app. If the tables fill the screen, they look like a plain old table view. But if we scroll them past their top or bottom bounds, we'll notice a total of four shadows: two on the outer boundaries of the view and two more tracking the top and bottom table cells. We're going to make a reusable table view that creates this same effect. Figure 23, *Table view border shadows*, on page 98 shows the look we're after.

Like in Recipe 19, *Produce Two-Tone Table Views*, on page 92, to do the job we'll override -layoutSubviews in a UITableView subclass. This time, though, we'll write a different layout algorithm to coordinate the shadows in all the appropriate places in the table.

The PRPShadowedTableView is a bit more complicated than the two-tone table we built previously: in that example, we had only two views to manage, and we simply stretched them to fill any gap made while scrolling beyond the top or bottom content bounds. Here, we're coordinating *four* subviews representing the shadows, with different conditions affecting each shadow.

Once again we're inserting subviews to represent the shadows. Why wouldn't we just set the shadows as part of the standard table header and footer? Well, first of all, doing this would affect the table's content size. If we set the bottom shadow as the table footer, for example, the table would include room at the bottom for the content shadow so that it was always visible. That isn't what we want: we want the shadows to have no effect on the actual content size and to be visible only when the respective top or bottom

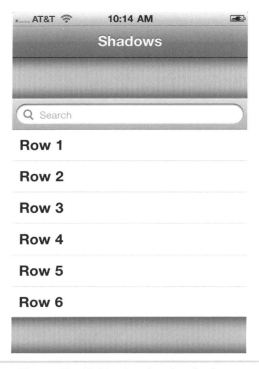

Figure 23—Table view border shadows

ends of the content are exposed. Second, we want this class to support custom headers and footers without affecting their layout or behavior. Using subviews that are independent of the other content gives us the greatest flexibility and safety.

We start with a common initializer that is called whether the table is created in code or in Interface Builder. This -commonInit method installs the four shadow views and performs some additional initialization.

ShadowedTables/Classes/PRPShadowedTableView.m
```
- (void)commonInit {
    [self installShadows];
}
```

The previously shown screenshot has a table view that doesn't fill the screen, making the bottom two shadows always visible. In the screenshot, the table is also pulled down past the top of its content, revealing the two top shadows as well. This shadow placement creates an appearance that resembles the Clock app.

The -installShadows method invoked by -commonInit initializes the four shadow views to use one of two shadow images. Both images are 1 pixel wide and safely stretchable to the left or right without any modifications. Each shadow view is then set up by the -installShadow: method for use in our table view. This step makes the shadows adaptable to any screen—iPhone, iPad, or whatever else comes along in the future.

ShadowedTables/Classes/PRPShadowedTableView.m

```
UIImage *upShadow = [UIImage imageNamed:@"shadowUp.png"];
UIImage *downShadow = [UIImage imageNamed:@"shadowDown.png"];
```

ShadowedTables/Classes/PRPShadowedTableView.m

```
- (void)installShadow:(UIImageView *)shadowView {
    shadowView.autoresizingMask = UIViewAutoresizingFlexibleWidth;
    CGRect contentFrame = shadowView.frame;
    contentFrame.size.width = self.frame.size.width;
    shadowView.frame = contentFrame;
    [self repositionShadow:shadowView];
}
```

Now that the shadow subviews are installed, we can work on positioning them. The easiest shadow to manage is the shadow above the top of the table's content. This shadow should freely move with the rest of the content but stay above the top while not actually affecting the content size. We accomplish this by setting a negative Y origin on the shadow. Since this never changes, we need to do it only once, so it's done early on from -installShadows.

ShadowedTables/Classes/PRPShadowedTableView.m

```
if (contentTopShadow == nil) {
    contentTopShadow = [[UIImageView alloc] initWithImage:upShadow];
    [self installShadow:contentTopShadow];
    CGRect topShadowFrame = contentTopShadow.frame;
    topShadowFrame.origin.y = -topShadowFrame.size.height;
    contentTopShadow.frame = topShadowFrame;
}
```

The fixed shadows at the top and bottom of the table view require some more work. When the user scrolls a scroll view or table view, all of the subviews move accordingly, unless we do something special in -layoutSubviews. Our -layoutSubviews implementation first passes the message on to super to preserve the default UITableView behavior and then sends -updateShadows to adjust the other three shadow views as needed.

ShadowedTables/Classes/PRPShadowedTableView.m

```
- (void)layoutSubviews {
    [super layoutSubviews];
    [self updateShadows];
}
```

First we update the fixed shadow at the top of the table. Because this subview would normally scroll with the rest of the content, we need to actively reposition it based on the scroll offset. We add an optimization to change the top shadow's position only if it's visible—that is, if the table's content offset is negative. A negative contentOffset.y value means we are pulling down on the table past the top edge.

ShadowedTables/Classes/PRPShadowedTableView.m
```
BOOL topShowing = (self.contentOffset.y < 0);
if (topShowing) {
    CGRect topFrame = self.topShadow.frame;
    topFrame.origin.y = self.contentOffset.y;
    self.topShadow.frame = topFrame;
    [self repositionShadow:self.topShadow];
    self.topShadow.hidden = NO;

    [self repositionShadow:self.contentTopShadow];
    self.contentTopShadow.hidden = NO;
} else {
    self.topShadow.hidden = YES;
    self.contentTopShadow.hidden = YES;
}
```

The next step, adjusting the bottom shadows, is a little trickier. Because table views receive -layoutSubviews so frequently, we only want to bother adjusting the shadows if they're showing. How do we know if the bottom shadows are exposed? We need to find out where the bottom of the table content is. "That's easy," you might be thinking. "Just get the last cell in the last section and get its frame; if it's nil, then the bottom clearly isn't showing." But what if the last section has no rows? What if we have twenty sections and the last three sections are empty? We could iterate backward until we find the row that is definitely last in the table, but doing this inside every call to -layoutSubviews is excessive.

OK, so using the "last cell" may not be reliable. What about the table's contentSize? If the table runs off the screen, contentSize.y is a valid metric. But it turns out that, depending on a table's contents, its contentSize may be the height of the table itself—even if the actual content is much smaller. So if we have a 460-pixel-high table with a search bar and a single 44-pixel row, contentSize.y could be reported as 460, not 44 as we might expect. See Figure 24, *Determining a table's content height*, on page 101 to understand the problem at hand.

It turns out UIKit already performs this measurement for us when it positions the table footer. If we have a table footer, we can just query its frame to find out the table's bottom Y coordinate.

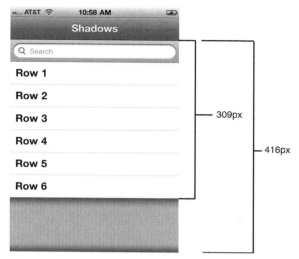

A table view's content height is always at least the height of the view itself. This table's contentSize.height is not 309 pixels as you might expect but rather 416. This makes determining the bottom shadow placement a little more difficult.

Figure 24—Determining a table's content height

What if we don't have a table footer? Easy: we insert one by overriding the -tableFooterView getter as a lazy initializer. If a footer is already installed, we just use that by messaging the superclass. If a footer is not installed, we insert a hidden, zero-height view as the footer. The setter is unchanged, so our view controller can replace the placeholder with a custom footer at any time. This gives us a dependable reference for the table's proper content height under any circumstances. If we need the placeholder, it's created only once, and not until the first -layoutSubviews message is received. This gives the calling code a chance to set a custom footer before the placeholder is created unnecessarily. Setting a footer also prevents placeholder separator lines from being drawn to the end of the view. You can see the effects in Figure 25, *Table footers to the rescue*, on page 102.

ShadowedTables/Classes/PRPShadowedTableView.m
```
- (UIView *)tableFooterView {
    UIView *footer = [super tableFooterView];
    if (footer == nil) {
        if (self.placeholderFooter == nil) {
            CGRect footerFrame = self.frame;
            footerFrame.size.height = 0;
            placeholderFooter = [[UIView alloc] initWithFrame:footerFrame];
```

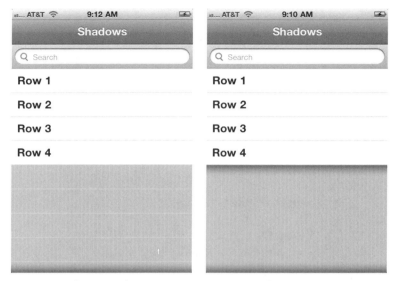

The presence of a table footer gives us reliable information on the end of a table's content so we know where to place our shadow. It also eliminates the "filler" separator lines drawn by plain table views.

Figure 25—Table footers to the rescue

```
    }
    self.placeholderFooter.hidden = YES;
    footer = self.tableFooterView = self.placeholderFooter;
  }

  return footer;
}
```

Once we know where the bottom of the table is, we decide whether to show or hide the bottom shadows and place them according to the gap between the table's static bottom and the bottom of the table's content.

```
ShadowedTables/Classes/PRPShadowedTableView.m
CGFloat footerMaxY = CGRectGetMaxY(self.tableFooterView.frame);
CGFloat bottomY = footerMaxY - self.contentOffset.y;
BOOL bottomShowing = (bottomY < self.frame.size.height);
if (bottomShowing) {
    CGFloat tableBottom = CGRectGetMaxY(self.frame);
    CGRect bottomFrame = self.bottomShadow.frame;
    CGFloat yOffset = (bottomFrame.size.height - self.contentOffset.y);
    CGFloat bottomY = tableBottom - yOffset;
    bottomFrame.origin.y = bottomY;
    self.bottomShadow.frame = bottomFrame;
```

> ## Editable Tables
>
> The table in this recipe is intended for read-only table views. Adding or deleting rows, either programmatically or in response to user-editing actions, is not addressed by the recipe. Properly handling edits requires you to anticipate the "new bottom" of the table, which adds a significant amount of complexity as this chapter suggests. We made a conscious decision for this book to keep the code simple and clean by only solving the noneditable case, which is still very common.

```
    [self repositionShadow:self.bottomShadow];
    self.bottomShadow.hidden = NO;

    CGRect cbFrame = self.contentBottomShadow.frame;
    cbFrame.origin.y = footerMaxY;
    self.contentBottomShadow.frame = cbFrame;
    [self repositionShadow:self.contentBottomShadow];
    self.contentBottomShadow.hidden = NO;
} else {
    self.bottomShadow.hidden = YES;
    self.contentBottomShadow.hidden = YES;
}
```

Finally, we send every shadow to the back in the -repositionShadow: method. We do this because as table cells are reused, their z-order varies. Pushing the shadows to the back ensures there won't be any strange cases where the shadow shows above normal table content. We additionally safeguard against the shadows clobbering table content by hiding them altogether based on the scroll position. Note that this code also accounts for the optional backgroundView property introduced in iOS 4.0.

ShadowedTables/Classes/PRPShadowedTableView.m
```
- (void)repositionShadow:(UIImageView *)shadowView {
    if (self.backgroundView) {
        [self insertSubview:shadowView aboveSubview:self.backgroundView];
    } else {
        [self insertSubview:shadowView atIndex:0];
    }
}
```

This self-contained class is ready for reuse from any view controller or codebase. You can set background colors, headers, and footers and still get all four shadows for free. As you've now seen in two examples, the -layoutSubviews method can help manage the situation with a small amount of code.

Recipe 21

Place Static Content in a Zoomable Scroll View

Problem

You want to create a zoomable scroll view with points that do not zoom with the main content, like the pins in the Maps app. This is not as straightforward as it sounds: depending on where you place your "pins," they either zoom with the content or move across the screen as the zoom scale changes.

Solution

UIScrollView makes it fairly easy to support arbitrary scrolling and zooming of content in your apps. This is all you have to do:

1. Set the minimum and maximum zoom scales to different values.

2. Set a delegate that specifies a content view for zooming.

Although simple, those steps are worth mentioning because they're often forgotten. Forgetting either one of them disables zooming for that scroll view. But that's not why we're here. We're here because we want to create static "pins," on our scroll view, just like Maps and MKMapView do. Figure 26, *Non-zooming scroll view content*, on page 105 shows an example of this effect.

Sounds simple, right? Not exactly. Let's take a look at our options, illustrated in the ScrollViewPins project. The ScrollViewPinsViewController includes a scroll view, for which it serves as the delegate. It returns an instance of PRPGridView—a simple class that draws a grid using UIBezierPath—as the view for zooming. This is all we need to enable zooming in our scroll view.

ScrollViewPins/Classes/Demo View Controllers/ScrollViewPinsViewController.m

```
- (UIView *)viewForZoomingInScrollView:(UIScrollView *)scrollView {
    return self.gridView;
}
```

All of the relevant connections between the views and view controller, as well as the required minimumZoomScale and maximumZoomScale values, are configured in ScrollViewPinsViewController.xib.

Now let's add some subviews. The project presents three tabs, each with a different subclass of ScrollViewPinsViewController that exhibits slightly different

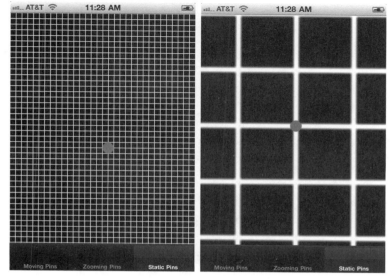

This recipe keeps select subviews in the same place and, at the same size, whenever the containing scroll view is zoomed.

Figure 26—Nonzooming scroll view content

behavior. Each view controller adds the same generated "pin view" to the screen but in significantly different ways. Run the project and take a look at how each tab differs, using two fingers (or drag in the Simulator with the option key held down) to zoom in and out.

The first tab adds the pin as a subview of the scroll view, independent of the grid we're zooming. This sounds intuitive because, as stated before, we want the pin to keep its dimensions as the grid content scales. Select the Moving Pins tab to see for yourself. Unfortunately, there's a wrinkle: the pin's size doesn't change as we zoom (good), but it does fly off the screen (bad). This "movement" occurs because the pin sits in the scroll view's coordinate space, which changes as zooming occurs.

Let's move on to the second tab, which adds the pin as a subview of the grid view—the view we're zooming within the scroll view. Select the Zooming Pins tab to see this view in action. We now have the opposite problem: the red pin no longer moves as the grid scales, but it now scales its size while zooming. This isn't what we want either. The scaling occurs because it was added as a subview of the grid, and the grid itself was scaled.

What we want is for the pin to stay still *and* stay the same size at all times. What's left to try?

First, let's discuss what happens when zooming occurs in a scroll view. As the user zooms on a scroll view, the scroll view's zoomScale property changes. As a result, the "zooming view" returned by -viewForZoomingInScrollView: receives a corresponding change to its transform property. The trick with transforms is that their effects are naturally inherited by subviews. This is why the pin in the Zooming Pins tab was scaling: our grid view, as the view for zooming, received a new transform that affected the pin's own scale.

Another thing that changes as zooming occurs is the scroll view's contentSize: larger as we zoom in; smaller as we zoom out. When the pin was a subview of the scroll view, set to an origin of, say, (10,10), that origin became a much less substantial dent in the content area as zooming occurred and the content size increased. This made it look like the pin in the Moving Pins tab was moving offscreen, when in fact we were simply focusing on a finer, more distant section of the scroll view's content.

So, how do we solve this problem? How do we get the benefits of both approaches but none of the drawbacks? The trick lies in the transform we mentioned earlier. If we could just invert the grid's transform and apply that inversion to the pins, then we could force the pins to stay their original size. Luckily, the CGAffineTransform API lets us do just that. So, we'll keep the pins as subviews of the grid and adjust its transform on the fly while zooming occurs.

But wait a minute. What if we have a complex hierarchy in our zooming view and we want only *some* of them to behave this way while the rest scale up and down along with everything else? We'll need a way to identify the nonzooming subviews. This is where PRPGridView's superclass, PRPScrollContentView, comes in. It's a very basic view that defines a set of subviews we want to keep static. These special "nonscaling" views will still be added as subviews, but they'll also be added to a set so we can keep track of which views we need to adjust.

ScrollViewPins/Classes/PRPScrollContentView.h
```
@interface PRPScrollContentView : UIView {}

@property (nonatomic, readonly, retain) NSMutableSet *nonScalingSubviews;

- (void)addNonScalingSubview:(UIView *)view;

@end
```

A convenience setter method, -addNonScalingSubview:, both adds the passed view to the hierarchy and flags it for exclusion from scaling, so our calling code doesn't need to remember both steps.

ScrollViewPins/Classes/PRPScrollContentView.m
```
- (void)addNonScalingSubview:(UIView *)view {
    [self.nonScalingSubviews addObject:view];
    [self addSubview:view];
}
```

With our subset of special views clearly defined, we go to work by overriding -setTransform: to call an adjustment routine for all of our nonscaling subviews.

ScrollViewPins/Classes/PRPScrollContentView.m
```
- (void)setTransform:(CGAffineTransform)transform {
    [super setTransform:transform];
    [self adjustSubviewsForTransform:transform];
}
```

This adjustment process is simple: invert the container's transform, which was set as a result of zooming, and apply that inverted transform to each subview we don't want scaled.

ScrollViewPins/Classes/PRPScrollContentView.m
```
- (void)adjustSubviewsForTransform:(CGAffineTransform)transform {
    CGAffineTransform inversion = CGAffineTransformInvert(transform);
    for (UIView *subview in self.nonScalingSubviews) {
        subview.transform = inversion;
    }
}
```

We wire up this new functionality by passing the pin view to -addNonScalingSubview: instead of -addSubview:. You can see this in the StaticPinsViewController class, and you can see the results by selecting the Static Pins tab in the demo app.

ScrollViewPins/Classes/Demo View Controllers/StaticPinsViewController.m
```
@implementation StaticPinsViewController

- (void)viewDidLoad {
    [super viewDidLoad];
    [self.gridView addNonScalingSubview:[self pinView]];
}

@end
```

Look closely as we zoom the view in this third tab: the pin does not resize itself, and it remains glued to its original point on the grid. How and why does this work? Well, let's say the scroll view was zoomed to 2x. This would apply a 2x scale transform to the grid view and, by association, all of its subviews. Inverting that transform gives us a one-half (0.5x) scale. By applying the 0.5x scale to our pins, we have an effective 1x scale (2.0 from the superview, multiplied by 0.5 from our adjustment code).

There are some other cool benefits to this solution that you might not appreciate. First, the pin remains centered along its original position. This is due to the fact that transforms applied to views (and their underlying layers) work off the center rather than the origin. Second, the transform inversion works in both directions, zooming both in and out. It even works during the "bounce" animation when we exceed the scroll view's minimum or maximum scale.

There are also some limitations. When using any of the animated UIScrollView zoom APIs, namely, -setZoomScale:animated: and -zoomToRect:animated:, the pins will not keep up with the animation—they momentarily scale along with the scroll view and quickly correct themselves when scrolling is over. This is because we don't have direct access to the animation machinery inside UIScrollView and therefore can't easily synchronize our own actions with it. This is a very small compromise that may not even be relevant to your application.

Recipe 22

Build a Carousel Paging Scroll View

Problem

You want to mimic the "carousel," round-robin paging behavior in Apple's Stocks app. You have a scroll view with a finite number of horizontal pages and need it to jump back around when scrolling past the end.

Solution

Jumping back around to the beginning or end of a list or array is pretty simple: just do some modulo arithmetic while adjusting your index, and you'll come back around once you move out of bounds. Applying this behavior to UIScrollView, and making that behavior work "infinitely," is a bit more complicated.

We'll solve this problem by building on top of Apple's PhotoScroller sample code from WWDC 2010. PhotoScroller demonstrates a number of interesting techniques on its own, including custom on-the-fly scroll view layout, tiled images, and reusable content views that work in a very similar fashion to table view cells. It's a great starting foundation for the work we need to do.

PhotoScroller comes with three images, each with its own dedicated "page" in the scroll view gallery. However, it displays those photos in a linear slideshow fashion. You can't scroll "backward" past the first image or "forward" beyond the last. In this recipe, we'll apply some extra logic to circle back around when scrolling past either end of the collection. This will create an "infinite" scrolling effect similar to what we see in the built-in Stocks app on iPhone. Figure 27, *Carousel behavior in a scroll view*, on page 110 illustrates this behavior.

Before we get into the logic of circling around, we need to figure out how to create the illusion of infinite horizontal scrolling. The key word here is illusion. Since scrolling is determined by our scroll view's contentSize property, we must have some finite value in place. What we'll do, then, is choose a particularly large value that the user is unlikely to scroll to either end of in casual usage. We've chosen a value of 500,000, stored it in a macro for this

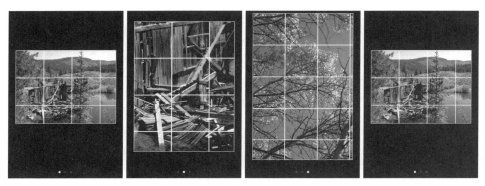

When paging past the last page, the scroll view comes right back around to the other side. It never stops at either end.

Figure 27—Carousel behavior in a scroll view

recipe, and used it in the modified -contentSizeForPagingScrollView method. This gives us about 1,000 pages of horizontal scrolling space.

```
- (CGSize)contentSizeForPagingScrollView {
    CGRect bounds = pagingScrollView.bounds;
    return CGSizeMake(kContentWidth, bounds.size.height);
}
```

The next thing we need to do is initialize our scroll view to start from the center, to prevent the user from hitting either the beginning or the end of the scroll boundaries anytime soon. We do this in -viewDidLoad by simply dividing the content width in half and setting that to a new contentOffset.

```
recycledPages = [[NSMutableSet alloc] init];
visiblePages  = [[NSMutableSet alloc] init];

pagingScrollView.contentSize = [self contentSizeForPagingScrollView];
CGFloat pageOffset = floorf(kContentWidth / 2);
pagingScrollView.contentOffset = CGPointMake(pageOffset, 0);
```

With these two changes in place, our scroll view now has infinite paging behavior. Feel free to enable the scroll view's horizontal scroll indicators to get a feel for just how much space we're working with: the indicator barely moves as you switch from page to page.

Now that our scroll area is sufficiently padded, it's time to tackle the primary task of circling the scroll view back around when we scroll past either end of our picture collection. We start with a small change to the -tilePages method.

PhotoScroller Sample Code

The PhotoCarousel project included with this book is a modified version of Apple's PhotoScroller sample. You can explore the original PhotoScroller project by searching for it in your Xcode documentation window and clicking Open Project.

In the original sample, the lastNeededPageIndex variable was compared to the last index of our image array to prevent us from running out of bounds. This is no longer a concern, since we're scrolling indefinitely and ultimately adjusting back around to the beginning of the array. But we definitely don't want to run past the edge of the *scroll view*, so we've done some quick math to make sure that doesn't happen.

PhotoCarousel/Classes/PhotoViewController.m
```
NSUInteger maxPage = (pagingScrollView.contentSize.width / visibleWidth);
lastNeededPageIndex  = MIN(lastNeededPageIndex, maxPage);
```

The next step is to figure out which of the three images to display when we're at, say, page 652 of our huge scroll view. We do this with a very basic change to the configurePage:forIndex: method. The original version of this method used the passed page index directly, and we simply do some modulo arithmetic on that (now huge) index before pulling one of our three images. This translates our arbitrarily large page index to something within the bounds of our image array.

PhotoCarousel/Classes/PhotoViewController.m
```
NSUInteger imageIndex = index % [self imageCount];
[page displayTiledImageNamed:[self imageNameAtIndex:imageIndex]
                        size:[self imageSizeAtIndex:imageIndex]];
```

Build and run PhotoCarousel to see these changes in action. We can now page left or right to our heart's content. When we go past the third image, we come back to the first. If we scroll backward beyond the first, we come back to the third. This goes on and on, seemingly forever. (It's not *actually* forever, but we'd have to page about 500 times in a single direction before realizing that.)

While playing with this project, you might notice the functional page control at the bottom of the screen. It updates accordingly as we move from page to page, and tapping on either side jumps backward and forward as we would expect. Let's see how that's wired up.

The page control is part of the XIB file and is set up as an IBOutlet in our PhotoViewController. The control is initially set up in -viewDidLoad right after the scroll view is initialized. We set the control's number of pages to the size of our image array and start it at page 0.

PhotoCarousel/Classes/PhotoViewController.m

```
pageControl.numberOfPages = [self imageCount];
pageControl.currentPage = 0;
[self scrollToPageIndex:0 animated:NO];
```

Note the -scrollToPageIndex:animated: message there. This method does some simple arithmetic to figure out the scroll view's current content offset and then conforms it to something that fits the requested image index. We send this message from -viewDidLoad and again in -pageControlTapped:, which is the action message we receive to handle taps on the page control. We can send this message at any other time to programmatically display one of our images at will.

PhotoCarousel/Classes/PhotoViewController.m

```
- (void)scrollToPageIndex:(NSInteger)pageIndex animated:(BOOL)animated
{
    CGPoint scrollOffset = pagingScrollView.contentOffset;
    CGFloat pageWidth = pagingScrollView.bounds.size.width;
    NSInteger currentPage = floorf(scrollOffset.x / pageWidth);
    NSInteger adjustedPage = currentPage % [self imageCount];
    NSInteger destinationPage = currentPage + (pageIndex - adjustedPage);
    scrollOffset.x = destinationPage * pageWidth;
    [pagingScrollView setContentOffset:scrollOffset animated:animated];
}
- (IBAction)pageControlTapped:(id)sender
{
    [self scrollToPageIndex:pageControl.currentPage animated:YES];
}
```

Finally, we need to programmatically update the page control's index in response to manual scrolling. We do this in -tilePages but not until a given page has filled the screen. We know this happens when the firstNeededPageIndex and lastNeededPageIndex variables are the same—in other words, when only one page is visible.

PhotoCarousel/Classes/PhotoViewController.m

```
if (firstNeededPageIndex == lastNeededPageIndex) {
    pageControl.currentPage = firstNeededPageIndex % [self imageCount];
}
```

There you have it: a paging scroll view that keeps on going, round and round, just like the Stocks app. The PhotoCarousel project, like its PhotoScroller predecessor, includes only three images, but you can easily add more to increase the number of displayable pages. You can also add your own custom views that do something completely different in each page.

CHAPTER 3

Graphics Recipes

The Graphics section presents recipes that focus primarily on a single application: Graphics Garden. Even though this is a simplistic example, we will explore techniques that you can apply to any application that requires dynamic visual components. Along the way, we take a look at the CALayer class and Core Animation libraries, which help you create dynamic and efficient visual effects.

The first six recipes in this section share sample code in the Graphics Garden application. Each recipe gradually moves you through the process of creating simple custom UIView objects, leading to more complex composite UIImageViews and eventually to a scene of multiple animated elements (see Figure 28, *The full Graphics Garden app*, on page 114). Wherever possible, we use Objective-C methods, but occasionally we need to drop down to C functions to access the lower-level Core Graphics libraries.

The last two recipes delve deeper into Core Animation, using the replicator layer to create a simple emitter and building an advanced transition using the power of sublayer transformation.

Figure 28—The full Graphics Garden app

Recipe 23

Draw Gradient-Filled Bezier Paths

Problem

To get the best-quality image at any size, you want to use Core Graphics to draw your objects. But Core Graphics C-based APIs can be cryptic and difficult to work with. Is there another way?

Solution

Before we dig into the code to draw our objects, it's worth taking a moment to review drawing in iOS. Custom drawing code is usually added to the drawRect: method of a UIView subclass. The drawRect: method is unusual in that it is never called directly from your code. It is triggered by the system to redraw the view contents whenever it thinks it is necessary, which in iOS is not often, because the views are backed by hardware-based layers. We can force a redraw by calling the setNeedsDisplay method. However, the redraw will not actually happen until the end of the run loop. A nice advantage of putting our drawing code in drawRect: is that we don't have to worry about initializing the graphics context (or drawing surface), though we can easily get a reference to it if we need it by calling the C function UIGraphicsGetCurrentContext.

The Core Graphics library provides a set of C functions that allows us to modify the graphic context properties, such as color and line thickness, and also to create points, lines, or curves that can then be *stroked* or drawn to the graphics context. We can also fill the area inside any drawn shape with the current color.

UIBezierPath, introduced in iOS 3.2, encapsulates much of the Core Graphics drawing functions into Cocoa methods and in doing so largely obviates the need to reference and manipulate graphics contexts. Unfortunately, in iOS, gradients still live very much in the world of C functions and contexts, but it is possible to make the two techniques work together (see Figure 29, *Shapes made from bezier curves*, on page 116).

We can use the UIBezierPath class to create a path from a series of lines or curves. An initial point is added first, and then each line is added to the end of the previous one. If we intend to fill the path, we must ensure that

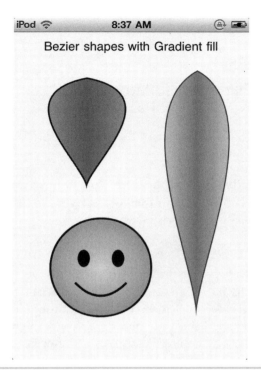

Figure 29—Shapes made from bezier curves

it is closed, either by adding a line that leads back to the start point or by using the closePath method. The really powerful feature of the UIBezierPath class is, as its name implies, the bezier curves. There are two methods we can use: addCurveToPoint:controlPoint1:controlPoint2: and addQuadCurveToPoint:controlPoint:. As you can see, the QuadCurve, or quadratic bezier, is the simpler of the two and requires only a single control point, whereas the default Curve, or cubic bezier, needs two control points but can create significantly more complex curves.[1]

A clipping path defines the area where the contents of the graphics context will be visible; anything outside of the path will not be rendered to the screen. A UIBezierPath can be made to act as a clipping path by calling the addClip method. In using this technique, a gradient, which would otherwise cover the entire view, will be rendered only inside the clip region defined by the edges of our shape.

---

1. For more on how bezier curves work, check out the UIBezierPath section of the iPad Programming Guide on http://developer.apple.com.

```
GraphicsGarden/PRPShapedView.m
-(CGGradientRef) gradientWithColor:(UIColor *)color
                           toColor:(UIColor *)color2
                             count:(CGFloat)colorCount
{
    const CGFloat *colorParts = CGColorGetComponents(color.CGColor);
    CGFloat red = colorParts[0];
    CGFloat green = colorParts[1];
    CGFloat blue = colorParts[2];

    const CGFloat *color2Parts = CGColorGetComponents(color2.CGColor);
    CGFloat red2 = color2Parts[0];
    CGFloat green2 = color2Parts[1];
    CGFloat blue2 = color2Parts[2];
    CGFloat graduations[] =
    {
        red, green, blue, 1.0,
        red2, green2, blue2, 1.0,
        red, green, blue, 1.0
    };

    CGColorSpaceRef rgb = CGColorSpaceCreateDeviceRGB();
    CGGradientRef gradient =
        CGGradientCreateWithColorComponents(rgb,
                                            graduations,
                                            NULL,
                                            colorCount);
    CGColorSpaceRelease(rgb);
    [(id)gradient autorelease];
    return gradient;
}
```

Each of our shapes shares a common set of attributes and methods, so it makes sense to break those elements out into a base class, PRPShapedView. This class declares several properties—lineThickness and strokeColor—as well as innerColor and outerColor properties, which are needed when we create the gradient. It also defines the gradientWithColor method, which creates the CGGradient based on the innerColor and outerColor properties.

The gradientWithColor method breaks up the UIColors into their RGB components and creates a C array containing three sets of components. (The fourth element of each set is the opacity, which we set to 1, opaque.) The first and third elements use the color parameter, and the middle element is set to color2. This gives us the flexibility to use the count to specify a gradient of the first two colors or three colors using the primary color as both the start and end color. From the CGGradient returned, each subclass can choose to render a linear or radial gradient in the view.

GraphicsGarden/PRPetal.m

```
- (void)drawRect:(CGRect)rect {

    CGFloat halfHeight = self.bounds.size.height/2;
    CGFloat halfWidth = self.bounds.size.width/2;
    CGFloat fullHeight = self.bounds.size.height;
    CGFloat fullwidth = self.bounds.size.width;

    CGPoint startPoint = CGPointMake(halfWidth, 3);
    CGPoint midPoint = CGPointMake(halfWidth, halfHeight*1.6);
    CGPoint endPoint = CGPointMake(halfWidth, fullHeight);
    CGPoint corner = CGPointMake(fullwidth, 0);
    CGPoint leftCtrl = CGPointMake(-halfWidth, halfHeight/3);
    CGPoint rightCtrl = CGPointMake(fullwidth*1.5, halfHeight/3);

    UIBezierPath *pPath = [UIBezierPath bezierPath];
    [pPath moveToPoint:startPoint];

    [pPath addCurveToPoint:endPoint
            controlPoint1:leftCtrl
            controlPoint2:midPoint];

    [pPath addCurveToPoint:startPoint
            controlPoint1:midPoint
            controlPoint2:rightCtrl];
    [pPath addClip];

    CGGradientRef gradient = [self gradientWithColor:self.innerColor
                                             toColor:self.outerColor
                                               count:3];
    CGContextRef context = UIGraphicsGetCurrentContext();
    CGContextDrawLinearGradient(context,
                                gradient,
                                CGPointZero,
                                corner,
                                0);
    pPath.lineWidth = self.lineThickness;
    [self.strokeColor setStroke];
    [pPath stroke];
}
```

Because the PRPetal class inherits from the base class PRPShapedView, we only need to override the drawRect: method. We build up the UIBezierPath from two cubic bezier curves that form the closed shape that we need to become a clipping Rect. The CGContextDrawLinearGradient function draws the gradient we created from the base class gradientWithColor method. Only then do we stroke the bezier path, clipping the gradient beneath it to match its shape.

```objc
- (void)drawRect:(CGRect)rect {

    CGFloat halfHeight = self.bounds.size.height/2;
    CGFloat halfWidth = self.bounds.size.width/2;
    CGFloat fullHeight = self.bounds.size.height;
    CGFloat fullwidth = self.bounds.size.width;
    CGFloat radius = (halfWidth > halfHeight) ? halfHeight : halfWidth;
    CGPoint midPoint = CGPointMake(halfWidth, halfHeight);

    UIBezierPath *pPath = [UIBezierPath
                bezierPathWithArcCenter: midPoint
                                 radius: radius
                             startAngle: 0
                               endAngle: M_PI*2
                              clockwise: YES];
    [pPath addClip];

    CGGradientRef gradient = [self gradientWithColor:self.innerColor
                                             toColor:self.outerColor
                                               count:2];

    CGContextRef context = UIGraphicsGetCurrentContext();

    CGContextDrawRadialGradient(context, gradient,
                                midPoint, 0,
                                midPoint, radius, 0);

    pPath.lineWidth = self.lineThickness*1.7;
    [self.strokeColor setStroke];
    [pPath stroke];

    // Eyes and Smile

    [pPath removeAllPoints];
    pPath.lineWidth = self.lineThickness;
    [pPath moveToPoint:CGPointMake(halfWidth/2, halfHeight*1.3)];
    [pPath addQuadCurveToPoint:CGPointMake(halfWidth*1.5, halfHeight*1.3)
              controlPoint:CGPointMake(halfWidth, fullHeight*.91)];
    [pPath stroke];

    pPath = [UIBezierPath
            bezierPathWithOvalInRect:CGRectMake(fullwidth/3-halfWidth*.1,
                                                fullHeight/3,
                                                halfWidth*.2,
                                                halfHeight*.3)];
    pPath.lineWidth = self.lineThickness;
    [pPath fill];
    [pPath stroke];
```

```
    pPath = [UIBezierPath
            bezierPathWithOvalInRect:CGRectMake(fullwidth/3*2-halfWidth*.1,
                                                fullHeight/3,
                                                halfWidth*.2,
                                                halfHeight*.3)];
    pPath.lineWidth = self.lineThickness;
    [pPath fill];
    [pPath stroke];
}
```

The PRPSmile class follows the pattern of the PRPetal class, except that we use an arc to draw a clipping circle, and we use the CGContextDrawRadialGradient function to create a radial gradient (colors radiate out from the center). The additional drawing code simply adds the eyes and smile to the graduated circle.

Now you have several views that you can use as building blocks for larger, more complex objects. In the next recipe, Recipe 24, *Create Dynamic Images with Multiple Animations*, on page 121, that's exactly what we'll do.

Recipe 24

Create Dynamic Images with Multiple Animations

Problem

Core Animation simplifies the process of animating an object, making it move, rotate, or change size. But now you want to combine those techniques to create a more complex effect. Where do you start?

Solution

Making an object pulse and spin may not be something you need to do every day, but the technique here demonstrates how you can easily create complex effects by applying multiple animations to a single object (see Figure 30, *Petals rotating and pulsing around the sun*, on page 122).

GraphicsGarden/PRPSunshine.m
```
UIView *shineView = [[UIView alloc] initWithFrame:self.bounds];
self.shineLayer = shineView.layer;
[self addSubview:shineView];
[shineView release];

for (CGFloat i = M_PI/10; i < M_PI*2; i += M_PI/7.5) {
    PRPetal *petal = [[PRPetal alloc] initWithFrame:petalRect];
    petal.outerColor = [UIColor yellowColor];
    petal.innerColor = [UIColor colorWithRed:1 green:.8 blue:.2 alpha:1];
    petal.lineThickness = 40;
    petal.strokeColor = [UIColor whiteColor];

    [shineView addSubview:petal];
    [petal release];
    petal.layer.anchorPoint = CGPointMake(.5, 2);
    petal.transform = CGAffineTransformMakeRotation(i);
}
[self addRotationAnimation];

PRPSmile *sunCenter = [[PRPSmile alloc] initWithFrame:sunRect];
sunCenter.innerColor = [UIColor yellowColor];
sunCenter.outerColor = [UIColor colorWithRed:1 green:.8 blue:.2 alpha:1];
[self addSubview:sunCenter];
[sunCenter release];
```

The PRPSunshine class creates the sun from the same components used in the previous recipes, PRPetal and PRPSmile. We modify the colors slightly for a

Figure 30—Petals rotating and pulsing around the sun

"sunnier" look and use a much thinner Rect for the petals. Here we also add the petals to a secondary UIView: shineView. shineView covers the same area as the main UIView but is used only to contain the petals. This allows us to add animation to the underlying layer without affecting the PRPSmile.

To create the circle of petals, we iterate through each of the required angles of rotation, in radians. A view will always rotate around its anchorPoint, which is usually set to the center of the Rect (0.5, 0.5). Because we need the petal to rotate around the center of the flower, rather than its own center, we need to set the anchorPoint to be below the lower edge of the Rect (0.5, 2). After that, a call to the CGAffineTransformMakeRotation method with the current radian value will ensure that the petal is positioned in the correct part of the flower and at the correct angle.

GraphicsGarden/PRPSunshine.m

```
CABasicAnimation *animation=[CABasicAnimation
                        animationWithKeyPath:@"transform.rotation"];
animation.duration=10;
animation.speed = self.animationSpeed;
animation.repeatCount = MAXFLOAT;
animation.fromValue=[NSNumber numberWithFloat:0];
animation.toValue= [NSNumber numberWithFloat:M_PI*2];
[self.shineLayer addAnimation:animation forKey:@"rotate"];

animation.keyPath = @"opacity";
animation.duration=.5;
animation.autoreverses = YES;
animation.fromValue=[NSNumber numberWithFloat:0.7];
```

```
animation.toValue= [NSNumber numberWithFloat:1.0];
[self.shineLayer addAnimation:animation forKey:@"fade"];

animation.keyPath = @"transform.scale";
animation.fromValue=[NSNumber numberWithFloat:.9];
animation.toValue= [NSNumber numberWithFloat:1.1];
[self.shineLayer addAnimation:animation forKey:@"scale"];
```

The three animations we are building in the addRotationAnimation method share many attributes, which means we can reuse the same animation object by simply modifying the properties that differ. Two of the animations are actually transformations that make use of CATransform3D, but because we are using Key-Path extensions, we do not need to construct the transformations ourselves. We can simply set the "from" and "to" values as NSNumbers, and the animation will construct the transformations for us. Using the Key-Path extensions comes with the added benefit of allowing the rotation to repeatedly turn a full circle. If we had used CATransform3D values for the rotation with the same angles, it would not have animated, because the starting angle and ending angle, 0 and 2*pi, respectively, would be effectively the same.

Adding the animation to a CALayer creates its own copy and further changes to that animation object have no effect on the CALayer. You can change any of the animation properties simply by adding an updated version. As long as you use the same key name for the new animation, you won't need to remove the old copy of the animation from the CALayer.

Recipe 25

Make Composited and Transformed Views

Problem

You want to build an image from components that you have already built, transforming some of the individual elements to get the look you want. How can you do that and still allow the resulting image to be efficiently animated?

Solution

The hierarchy of UIViews allows us to layer multiple components to build up an image. We can create complex results by modifying the properties of each of the independent subviews. Once all of the UIViews are in place, we can then use a few lines of Core Graphics code to composite those UIViews into a single image.

As part of the Graphics Garden app, we use this technique to construct the flower image. We create the flower by using the basic elements we built in Recipe 23, *Draw Gradient-Filled Bezier Paths*, on page 115. It consists of a ring of petals with a central smiley face and a short stem, with two additional petals shaded green to indicate leaves growing out from the stem.

This code constructs the composite UIView piece by piece from the component classes we have already created.

GraphicsGarden/PRPFlower.m
```
CGFloat halfHeight = self.bounds.size.height/2;
CGFloat halfWidth = self.bounds.size.width/2;
CGFloat fullHeight = self.bounds.size.height;
CGFloat fullwidth = self.bounds.size.width;
CGRect smileRect = CGRectMake(halfWidth/2, halfHeight/4*.9,
                              halfWidth, halfHeight);
CGRect petalRect = CGRectMake(halfWidth-fullwidth/10, fullHeight/5,
                              fullwidth/5, fullwidth/2);
CGRect leafRect = CGRectMake(halfWidth-fullwidth/12, fullHeight*.84,
                             fullwidth/5, fullwidth/2);
CGRect stemRect = CGRectMake(halfWidth-fullwidth/8, halfHeight*1.3,
                             fullwidth/4, halfHeight*.8);

PRPStem *stem = [[PRPStem alloc] initWithFrame:stemRect];
stem.outerColor = [UIColor colorWithRed:0 green:.5 blue:0 alpha:1];
stem.innerColor = [UIColor colorWithRed:0.3 green:1 blue:.2 alpha:1];
```

```
[self addSubview:stem];
[stem release];

for (CGFloat i = M_PI/10; i < M_PI*2; i += M_PI/7.5) {
    PRPetal *petal = [[PRPetal alloc] initWithFrame:petalRect];
    petal.outerColor = [UIColor purpleColor];
    petal.innerColor = [UIColor colorWithRed:1 green:0 blue:1 alpha:1];
    [self addSubview:petal];
    [petal release];
    petal.layer.anchorPoint = CGPointMake(.5, 1);
    petal.transform = CGAffineTransformMakeRotation(i);
}

for (CGFloat i = -M_PI/5; i < M_PI/5; i += M_PI/5*2) {
    PRPetal *leaf = [[PRPetal alloc] initWithFrame:leafRect];
    leaf.outerColor = [UIColor colorWithRed:0 green:.5 blue:0 alpha:1];
    leaf.innerColor = [UIColor colorWithRed:0.3 green:1 blue:.2 alpha:1];
    [self addSubview:leaf];
    [leaf release];
    leaf.layer.anchorPoint = CGPointMake(.5, 1);
    leaf.transform = CGAffineTransformMakeRotation(i);
}

PRPSmile *smile = [[PRPSmile alloc] initWithFrame:smileRect];
smile.innerColor = [UIColor yellowColor];
smile.outerColor = [UIColor colorWithRed:1 green:.4 blue:0 alpha:1];
[self addSubview:smile];
[smile release];
```

To keep the process simple, we add the subviews, starting from the rearmost UIView, and build up the flower as each part is added. In this case, the stem is added first based on the PRPStem class. The outer ring of the flower is formed as each petal is added to the UIView, pointing up from the center, and transformed using CGAffineTransformMakeRotation with an incrementing angle of rotation (specified here as a fraction of Pi). The anchorPoint property is crucial here, because that defines the center of rotation for our transformation. The two leaves are then added using the same technique but with a much smaller range of rotation and an offset starting angle. Finally, the PRPSmile object is added to the UIView with its center set to match the center of rotation of the petals.

Now that we have the code to create the flower, we could use it to create all the flowers we need in our scene, but that would result in numerous UIViews. Apart from the large memory footprint, the total time needed to instantiate so many UIViews would be quite significant.

Only one PRPFLower object is created here, even though we are placing sixty flowers in our scene, because an image is created from that object using the new category method PRPCompositeView.

GraphicsGarden/MainViewController.m

```
PRPFlower *flower = [[PRPFlower alloc] initWithFrame:flowerRect];
UIImage *compositeFlower = [flower PRPCompositeView];
[flower release];

for (int i = 0; i < 60; i++) {
    int size = height/12;
    CGFloat flowerSize = arc4random()%size+size;
    CGRect flowerRect = CGRectMake(arc4random()%(int)width*0.9,
                                   arc4random()%pos+2*pos ,
                                   flowerSize*0.7,
                                   flowerSize);
    UIImageView *compView = [[UIImageView alloc] initWithFrame:flowerRect];
    compView.image = compositeFlower;
    compView.layer.zPosition = flowerRect.origin.y+flowerSize;
    [self.view addSubview:compView];
    [compView release];
    [self growUp:compView forDuration:arc4random()%100/25.0+4];
}
```

We can then build out our scene by creating UIImageViews based on our new image. With each flower being a single entity, they can be individually animated, which wouldn't have been possible had it still been a hierarchy of UIViews.

Here's the code for the category method we need to composite our image from multiple UIViews:

GraphicsGarden/UIView+PRPCompositedView.m

```
UIGraphicsBeginImageContextWithOptions(self.layer.bounds.size, NO, 0);
[self.layer renderInContext:UIGraphicsGetCurrentContext()];
UIImage *compoundImage = UIGraphicsGetImageFromCurrentImageContext();
UIGraphicsEndImageContext();

return compoundImage;
```

The CALayer method renderInContext is key, because it renders *all* sublayers into the graphics context, effectively flattening our hierarchy into a single element. The C method UIGraphicsGetImageFromCurrentImageContext() uses the bitmap data from the graphics context and builds the new UIImage.

By using rotation transformation, we avoid the need to create more complex components for our image. Compositing our UIViews into a single UIImage allows us to reduce memory usage, increase performance, and animate the flower.

Recipe 26

Animate a Gradient Layer

Problem

Adding background gradients can greatly improve the presentation of a view that would otherwise be rendered in a single solid color. But you want to go further and give your gradients a dynamic element to indicate a change of state or to show that the app is responding to user input.

Solution

The CALayer family of classes has grown in the last few releases of iOS, pulling in many of the classes previously found only in Mac OS X. With iOS 3.0, Apple introduced CAGradientLayer, making it easy for you to generate a graduated background for any UIView. The greatest advantage of using this class comes from the animatable properties, which can create extremely fast, hardware-based effects. Animation even extends to the arrays of colors used to build the gradients, so you can create a smooth, interpolated, cross-fade of gradients (see Figure 31, *Animated gradient layer*, on page 128). The only downside of CAGradientLayer is that currently you can use only an axial, or linear, gradient.[2]

Using this technique yields a nicely animated opening fade-in of a multicolored graduated background, demonstrated in the context of the Graphics Garden sample app. You could apply this to create an animated sunrise-sunset effect, for example.

Although we are using CAGradientLayer, we add our code to a UIView subclass. That may not seem intuitive, but remember that each UIView is backed by a CALayer, and by overriding the layerClass method we can ensure this view is backed by a CAGradientLayer.

GraphicsGarden/GradientView.m
```
+ (Class)layerClass {
    return [CAGradientLayer class];
}
```

---

2. The Core Graphics libraries can create a radial, or circular, gradient, so there may be hope for the future.

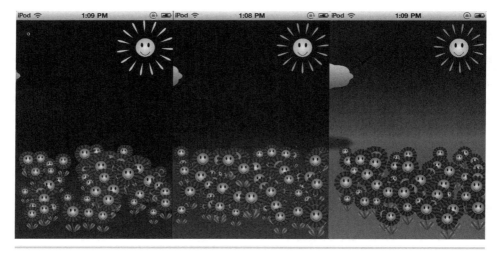

Figure 31—Animated gradient layer

Overriding the layerClass method is a technique more often used for OpenGL-backed UIViews, but it works just as well for creating the gradient-backed UIView we need here.

First we set up the initial color array to reflect how we want the gradient to look at the end of the animation. This code initializes the values that fix the three main colors to their relative positions in the UIView to give the overall effect we want. Without these control values, the generated gradient would have the colors spaced evenly throughout the layer.

GraphicsGarden/GradientView.m
```
- (void)didMoveToSuperview {
    self.backgroundColor = [UIColor blackColor];
    CGColorRef color = [UIColor blackColor].CGColor;
    UIColor *color1 = [UIColor colorWithRed:0.01 green:0.20 blue:0.80
                                                          alpha:1.0];
    UIColor *color2 = [UIColor colorWithRed:1.00 green:0.50 blue:0.00
                                                          alpha:1.0];
    UIColor *color3 = [UIColor colorWithRed:0.35 green:0.74 blue:0.11
                                                          alpha:1.0];
    NSArray *colors = [NSArray arrayWithObjects:(id)[color1 CGColor],
                       [color2 CGColor],
                       [color3 CGColor],
                       nil];

    CAGradientLayer *gLayer = (CAGradientLayer *)self.layer;
    gLayer.colors = colors;
    gLayer.locations = [NSArray arrayWithObjects:
                        [NSNumber numberWithFloat:0.0],
```

```
                          [NSNumber numberWithFloat:0.4],
                          [NSNumber numberWithFloat:0.9],
                          nil];
        gLayer.startPoint = CGPointMake(0.5, 0);
        gLayer.endPoint = CGPointMake(0.5, 1);
```

The animation code should be starting to look familiar; it follows the standard pattern of a CABasicAnimation setup. We could have used a CAAnimationGroup to ensure that the two animations run concurrently, but the result would be the same because they share the same duration and timing function.

GraphicsGarden/GradientView.m

```
CABasicAnimation *anim = [CABasicAnimation animationWithKeyPath:
                                              @"startPoint"];
anim.fromValue = [NSValue valueWithCGPoint:CGPointMake(0.5, 1)];
anim.duration = Duration
anim.timingFunction = [CAMediaTimingFunction
                  functionWithName:kCAMediaTimingFunctionEaseOut];
[gLayer addAnimation:anim forKey:@"start"];

anim = [CABasicAnimation animationWithKeyPath:@"colors"];
anim.fromValue = [NSArray arrayWithObjects:(id)color, color, color, nil];
anim.duration = Duration;
anim.timingFunction = [CAMediaTimingFunction
                  functionWithName:kCAMediaTimingFunctionEaseOut];
[gLayer addAnimation:anim forKey:@"colors"];
```

The first animation object applies to the Startpoint property, which sets the start position of the gradient, specified in unit coordinates, transitioning from 1.0 (bottom of view) to 0 (top of view). This produces the effect of a gradual rise up the screen. Adding a kCAMediaTimingFunctionEaseOut timing function causes the animation to start quickly and then transition to a slower stop.

The second animation block drives the change of color. When the animation object is built, only the fromValue needs to be set to the array of colors from which we want the transition to begin—in this case, all black. The animation object interpolates to the colors currently stored in the layer. This technique would not work if we were adding the animation object after the view had already been rendered, because the gradient would appear in full, then disappear, and then animate back into view.

GraphicsGarden/MainViewController.m

```
GradientView *gradView = [[GradientView alloc] initWithFrame:
                                              self.view.bounds];
[self.view addSubview:gradView];
[gradView release];
```

Adding the GradientView to the main view, as shown here, does two things. First, the GradientView becomes a subview of the main background view, and second, it triggers the initialization and animation of the underlying gradient layer. We get this result because we placed the code for those functions in the didMoveToSuperview delegate method. This method is called only when the addSubview method is called—the advantage being that the instantiation of the gradientView is separated from its activation, so we avoid any issues with timing the animation. If we had added gradient code to the initWithFrame method, it's possible that the animation would have started before the view was rendered.

You can use this technique to create quite complex gradients, because you can specify as many colors and control points as you want. By modifying the animation timing, along with the start or end color arrays, you can produce a variety of eye-catching effects.

Could you have done this another way? Filling a view with a gradient is relatively simple, as you saw in Recipe 23, *Draw Gradient-Filled Bezier Paths*, on page 115. But without this technique, animating that gradient, especially getting the cross-fade effect, would require a lot more code and be a great deal more processor-intensive.

Recipe 27

Reshape Shadows

Problem

You can add the impression of depth to any view simply by including a shadow, and in most cases that addition is all you need to produce the desired effect. But what if you want to render a shadow that doesn't follow the shape of the image in the view, perhaps to imply the angle of the source of light or to render the shape of the ground the shadow is passing over. How can you modify the shadow's shape to create these or similar effects?

Solution

You can define a CALayer to display a shadow that follows its nontransparent shape, offset from the image contents, to give the effect of the view being shown in relief, set apart from the background. Apple introduced a new property in iOS 3.2 that defines a shadowPath. This path does not need to follow the shape of the CALayer contents, so we can be a little more creative and go beyond the default relief shadow. In this case, we will build a cloud image that appears to cast its flattened shadow on the ground as it floats across the screen.

GraphicsGarden/PRPCloud.m
```
- (void)drawRect:(CGRect)rect {
    CGFloat fullHeight = self.bounds.size.height;
    CGPoint top = CGPointMake(0, 0);
    CGPoint bottom = CGPointMake(0, fullHeight);
    UIBezierPath *pPath = [self CreatePathWithHeight:
                                            self.bounds.size.height];
    [pPath addClip];
    CGGradientRef gradient = [self gradientWithColor:self.innerColor
                                            toColor:self.outerColor
                                            count:2];
    CGContextRef context = UIGraphicsGetCurrentContext();
    CGContextDrawLinearGradient(context,
                            gradient,
                            top,
                            bottom,
                            0);
    pPath.lineWidth = self.lineThickness;
```

```
[self.strokeColor setStroke];
[pPath stroke];
pPath = [self CreatePathWithHeight:self.bounds.size.height/2.0];
self.layer.shadowPath = pPath.CGPath;
if (!self.shadowDistance) shadowDistance = self.bounds.size.height*1.8;
self.alpha = 0.9;
self.layer.shadowOffset = CGSizeMake(0, self.shadowDistance);
self.layer.shadowOpacity = 0.4;
}
```

PRPCloud is a subclass of PRPShapedView and therefore follows the same pattern as all the simple view objects in the Graphics Garden application. In the drawRect method, we build our cloud image using a UIBezierPath that is created in CreatePathWithHeight (shown next) from a C array of relative points. The CreatePathWithHeight method uses the height parameter to adjust the position of the points as the path is built.

GraphicsGarden/PRPCloud.m

```
- (UIBezierPath *) CreatePathWithHeight:(CGFloat)h {
    CGFloat w = self.bounds.size.width;
    CGFloat points[] =
    {
                0.4, 0.2,
        0.5, 0.1, 0.6, 0.2,
        0.8, 0.2, 0.8, 0.4,
        0.9, 0.5, 0.8, 0.6,
        0.8, 0.8, 0.6, 0.8,
        0.5, 0.9, 0.4, 0.8,
        0.2, 0.8, 0.2, 0.6,
        0.1, 0.5, 0.2, 0.4,
        0.2, 0.2, 0.4, 0.2,
    };

    CGPoint point;
    CGPoint cPoint;
    UIBezierPath *pPath = [UIBezierPath bezierPath];

    point = CGPointMake(points[0]*w, points[1]*h);
    [pPath moveToPoint:point];

    for (int i = 2; i < sizeof(points)/sizeof(float); i+=4) {
        cPoint = CGPointMake(points[i]*w, points[i+1]*h);
        point = CGPointMake(points[i+2]*w, points[i+3]*h);

        [pPath addQuadCurveToPoint:point controlPoint:cPoint];
    }
    [pPath closePath];

    return pPath;
}
```

Consequently, we need to call the CreatePathWithHeight in two places—first to create the path for the cloud and then for the shadowPath property but with half the original height. The shadowOffset of the layer is set to the value of the shadowDistance property of the cloud view, placing it far enough below the cloud to give the impression that it's at ground level.

You could also create a shadow using an additional CALayer, but that would require the extra step of synchronizing the position of the two layers whenever you needed to move or animate them.

Recipe 28

Display Animated Views

Problem

You can use Core Graphics to create a series of UIImageViews that represent various stages of a moving object. How do you display them in sequence to create a looping animation?

Solution

We've addressed animation in some detail in the recipes in this section, working mostly with manipulating the position or rotation of layers. Classic cell animation, like the kind seen in cartoons, uses a different technique that involves displaying a sequence of images that fool the brain into seeing continuous movement. We can create the same visual effect by providing an instance of the UIImageView class with an array of images. Normally, we create these images offline and then load them from file, but in this case, we will follow our previous examples and create our images using the now-familiar Core Graphics techniques.

To keep the artwork simple, we will build the classic line-drawn seagull animation, with the two wings seeming to flap up and down as the body bounces between them (see Figure 32, *Frames of the seagull animation*, on page 135). To render the wings of our bird, we just need a pair of quadratic bezier curves.

The PRPBird class extends the UIImageView class to build and assign our array of images.

GraphicsGarden/PRPBird.m
```
- (void)didMoveToSuperview {

    if (!self.animationImages) {
        self.animationImages = [self arrayOfFrames];
    }
}
```

To ensure that the UIImageView has been added to the main view before we build our images, we override the didMoveToSuperview method to assign the array to the animationImages property.

Figure 32—Frames of the seagull animation

GraphicsGarden/PRPBird.m
```
- (NSArray *)arrayOfFrames {

    NSMutableArray *imageArray = [NSMutableArray arrayWithCapacity:COUNT];

    for (CGFloat i = LOWWING; i < HIGHWING; i+=STEPS) {
        [imageArray addObject:[self animationFrame:i]];
    }
    for (CGFloat i = HIGHWING; i > LOWWING; i-=STEPS) {
        [imageArray addObject:[self animationFrame:i]];
    }

    return [NSArray arrayWithArray:imageArray];
}
```

The arrayOfFrames method builds up the NSMutableArray of images by looping through two sets of calls to the animationFrame, where the wings are drawn. The parameter i relates to the height of the edge of each wing. We use two separate loops here because we need to generate all of the frames for our animation—both the wings flapping downward and the wings flapping back up again. Because the animation automatically repeats, it will give the impression of continuous movement.

GraphicsGarden/PRPBird.m
```
- (UIImage *)animationFrame:(CGFloat)frameNum {

    CGFloat width = self.bounds.size.width;
    CGFloat height = self.bounds.size.height;

    UIGraphicsBeginImageContextWithOptions(CGSizeMake(width, height),
                                                      NO, 0);
    UIBezierPath *path = [UIBezierPath bezierPath];

    [path moveToPoint:CGPointMake(0, frameNum)];
    [path addQuadCurveToPoint:CGPointMake(0.5, 0.6-frameNum/3)
                controlPoint:CGPointMake(0.25, 0.25)];
    [path addQuadCurveToPoint:CGPointMake(1, frameNum)
                controlPoint:CGPointMake(0.75, 0.25)];
```

```
    [path applyTransform:CGAffineTransformMakeScale(width, height)];

    path.lineWidth = height/30;
    [path stroke];

    UIImage *frameImage = UIGraphicsGetImageFromCurrentImageContext();

    UIGraphicsEndImageContext();

    return frameImage;
}
```

With our recipes so far, we've always placed drawing code in the drawRect: method, but here we're actually building a series of fixed images, so we need to use a different technique. We will create our own graphics context by calling the Core Graphics function, UIGraphicsBeginImageContextWithOptions(). UIBezierPath uses the default context, in this case the one we just created. The two curves are added to the path, varying the start points and end points a little for each frame. Using the UIGraphicsGetImageFromCurrentImageContext() method, a UIImage is built from our context and passed back to be added to the array.

GraphicsGarden/MainViewController.m
```
CGRect rect = CGRectMake(-width/5, width/8, width/8, height/8);
PRPBird *bird = [[PRPBird alloc] initWithFrame:rect];
[self.view addSubview:bird];
[bird release];
bird.animationDuration = 1.0;
[bird startAnimating];

CABasicAnimation *birdAnim = [CABasicAnimation animation];
birdAnim.keyPath = @"position";
CGPoint birdPos = CGPointMake(width, bird.center.y*2);
birdAnim.toValue = [NSValue valueWithCGPoint:birdPos];
birdAnim.duration = DURATION/2;
birdAnim.repeatCount = MAXFLOAT;
[bird.layer addAnimation:birdAnim forKey:@"pos"];
```

Using the PRPBird class is no different from using a regular UIImageView, except that the animation array is prepopulated. The animationDuration property controls the speed of our animation, and there are methods to start and stop it as required. To give the impression that our seagull is flying, we create an animation object to animate its position from one side of the main view to the other.

By using your own graphics context, you're able to draw the objects you need and easily build a series of images that can be animated in sequence.

Discussion

Could you get the same result some other way? Sure—you could use an NSTimer, changing the contents of the view each time the timer fires, but because the timer is triggered by the run loop, the potential for delays is greater than with UIView animation, which runs in its own thread.

Recipe 29

Construct a Simple Emitter

Problem

A particle emitter has various uses in a graphical application—for example, as a background visual or as a dynamic component of a larger view. It would be nice if a particle emitter were available on iOS, but currently this feature is available only on Mac OS X. If you wanted to build one yourself, you would normally need to descend into OpenGL. Is it possible to create a simple emitter using only Core Animation?

Solution

We can create a simple emitter using Core Animation, but to get reasonable performance, we need to consider how best to do it. An emitter is usually required to handle a large number of particles, each of them being a distinct graphic element. Though we could use Core Animation to create a layer for each particle, this would be very expensive in terms of both memory and GPU time. The processor time needed to instantiate a large number of layers could also be a limiting factor.

An alternate solution then would be for us to use a combination of the CAReplicatorLayer class and CABasicAnimation. The CAReplicatorLayer class is a little-used subclass of CALayer that uses the GPU to create exact duplicates of the contents of the original layer, while varying some of the properties by small incremental changes as each copy is rendered. Only the sublayers of the replicator layer are duplicated, so we must always include a source layer, or layers, that contains the visual elements.

For example, using a CAReplicatorLayer, we could create a line of images, each an exact copy of the original, by setting the contents of the main sublayer to the image; setting the instanceTransform to, say, 10 points of X translation; and setting the instanceCount to 10. This would create a line of 10 duplicate images all 10 points apart—useful, but not quite what we want (see Figure 33, *Four separate instances of the simple emitter*, on page 139).

To create the emitter effect, we need to animate the position of the image sublayer. As the sublayer moves, each of its duplicates also moves so that

Figure 33—Four separate instances of the simple emitter

we now have a moving line of images. By adding another component, in-stanceDelay, we can really augment this effect because each duplicate element is added only after that specified delay. A fraction of a second is enough to create the kind of effect we want.

We create a new class, PRPSimpleEmitterLayer, which is a subclass of CAReplicator-Layer, to add the coordinated animation to the base class. In the init method, we add our sublayer and set its contents to the default image, in this case a small bright spark.

SimpleEmitter/SimpleEmitter/PRPSimpleEmitterLayer.m

```
- (id)init {
    self = [super init];
    if (self) {
        self.count = 1;
        self.instanceColor = [UIColor whiteColor].CGColor;
        imageLayer = [CALayer layer];
        self.imageLayer.contents =
                (id)[UIImage imageNamed:@"tspark.png"].CGImage;
        [self addSublayer:self.imageLayer];
    }
    return self;
}
```

The start method configures the properties for the imageLayer and the replicator layer, based on any modified properties from the view controller. We calculate the instanceDelay from the cycleTime and the count, spreading out the duplicated elements evenly for the duration of the animation.

The incremental property, rotator, is the angle of rotation added to each subsequent replicated imagelayer and will result in spiraling the particles as they are emitted, giving quite a nice effect. We rotate the imagelayer itself by angle degrees (in radians) so that we can emit the particles in any desired direction.

SimpleEmitter/SimpleEmitter/PRPSimpleEmitterLayer.m

```
- (void)start {

    self.imageLayer.frame = self.bounds;
    self.imageLayer.opacity = 1.0;
    self.instanceCount = count;
    self.instanceDelay = cycleTime/count;
    CATransform3D t = CATransform3DMakeRotation(self.rotator, 0, 0, 1);
    self.instanceTransform = CATransform3DTranslate(t,
                                                    xAdjust,
                                                    yAdjust, 0);
    self.transform = CATransform3DMakeRotation(angle, 0, 0, 1);

    [self animate];
}
```

We use a now-familiar CABasicAnimation object to animate the position of the imagelayer. We only need be concerned with distance of movement at this point, because we later rotate the imagelayer to point the emitted particles in any direction we want. So, the newPoint value need only be based on the length property.

SimpleEmitter/SimpleEmitter/PRPSimpleEmitterLayer.m

```
-(void)animate {

    CGPoint newPoint = CGPointMake(0, length);
    CABasicAnimation *basic = [CABasicAnimation animation];
    basic.keyPath = @"position";
    basic.toValue = [NSValue valueWithCGPoint:newPoint];
    basic.duration = self.cycleTime;
    basic.repeatCount = MAXFLOAT;
    [imageLayer addAnimation:basic forKey:@"position"];
}
```

Stopping the emitter simply involves removing the animation and setting the imageLayer opacity to zero.

SimpleEmitter/SimpleEmitter/PRPSimpleEmitterLayer.m

```
- (void)stop {

    self.imageLayer.opacity = 0;
    self.instanceCount = 0;
    [self.imageLayer removeAllAnimations];
}
```

Setting up an emitter from the view controller looks a lot more complicated than it is. We instantiate the layer just like any other and set its origin to act as the center of the emitter and its frame size to the size of the particle. With the combination of the properties from the replicator layer and the new properties on the simple emitter layer, we have a lot of values we can play with to create different effects. In the SimpleEmitterViewController class, we have a set of emitter methods, each of which produces quite different results. emitter1 produces a spiral effect because it defines an incremental rotator angle, which needs to be quite small because we have 100 "particles." We also modify the color slightly for each particle by setting the instanceGreenOffset property to a small negative value, slowly reducing the green element of the color; we do the same for the red and blue elements.

SimpleEmitter/SimpleEmitter/SimpleEmitterViewController.m

```
-(PRPSimpleEmitterLayer *)emitter1 {

    CGFloat w = self.view.frame.size.width;
    CGFloat h = self.view.frame.size.height;
    PRPSimpleEmitterLayer *emitter =
                        [PRPSimpleEmitterLayer layer];
    emitter.frame = CGRectMake(w/4, h/2, 16,16);
    emitter.rotator = -M_PI*4/50;
    emitter.length = w/4;
    emitter.count = 100;
    emitter.angle = 2.5;
    emitter.cycleTime = 1.0;
    emitter.instanceGreenOffset = -0.1/emitter.count;
    emitter.instanceRedOffset = -0.5/emitter.count;
    emitter.instanceBlueOffset = -0.1/emitter.count;
    [self.view.layer addSublayer:emitter];
    return emitter;
}
```

In the emitter4 method, we also override the instanceColor value to set the particle to red and set the sublayer image to a BrightBlob image instead of the default spark.

```
-(PRPSimpleEmitterLayer *)emitter4 {

    CGFloat w = self.view.frame.size.width;
    CGFloat h = self.view.frame.size.height;
    PRPSimpleEmitterLayer *emitter =
                        [PRPSimpleEmitterLayer layer];
    emitter.frame = CGRectMake(0, h, 16,16);
    emitter.rotator = 0.02;
    emitter.length = w;
    emitter.count = 6;
    emitter.angle = 4.0;
    emitter.cycleTime = 1.6;
    emitter.instanceColor = [UIColor redColor].CGColor;
    emitter.imageLayer.contents =
                (id)[UIImage imageNamed:@"brightBlob.png"].CGImage;

    [self.view.layer addSublayer:emitter];
    return emitter;
}
```

The four samples in the view controller show how making small changes to
the various properties of the emitter creates dramatically different effects:
spirals, pulsing, and simulated gunfire. You could create more effects by
adding additional rotation animation to the emitter or by adding additional
replicator layers as sublayers to the main layer and animating those inde-
pendently. While you wait for CAEmitterLayer to move down to iOS from OS X,
this simple emitter can provide some of that functionality.

Recipe 30

Curl the Page to a New View

Problem

Simulating a page turn is a popular visual technique, often used in book- or magazine-reading apps. Creating a realistic effect, such as the one used in iBooks, requires detailed knowledge of OpenGL. Is it possible to create a similar effect using only the higher-level Core Animation APIs?

Solution

The Core Animation APIs encompass a great deal of functionality including layer manipulation and various styles of animation, but hidden in their depths is a relatively unknown feature called *sublayer transformation*. We've shown in several recipes how you can transform a layer in many ways—through scaling, rotation, and translation. Sublayer transformation gives us the same level of control but over the entire layer hierarchy. If you combine this technique with rotations that take into account depth in the z-axis, you can effectively control objects in a 3D space. This is the technique we will use to implement our transition (see Figure 34, *A partial page curl transition*, on page 145).

We first need to split the transitioning view into a series of layer strips; by making use of the PRPCompositedView category, we can ensure that the view and any subviews it may have get composited into a single image before we break it into strips.

We also need to create a second set of layers the same size as the image strips but initially without any contents so they will be completely transparent. We attach this set of strips as sublayers to our transforming layer. Each of these strips is added with an incrementing amount of rotation and translation applied, effectively creating a multisided tube. If we were to look at this tube in cross section, the center point of the multisided shape would match the center point of the parent layer. By using sublayer transformation, rotating the parent layer will result in the tube rotating about its center. If we simultaneously animate the tube from one side of the screen to the other while gradually replacing the contents of the strips with the image strips of the original view, it will appear as if the view is curling away from the background.

It's probably worth running the sample app at this point to get a sense of how the transition works, but we will need to dig into the code to really understand the mechanics of the process.

The viewWithView class method creates the instance of the PRPViewTransition class and uses the PRPCompositedView category to composite the specified view with its subViews into a single image that can be split into the requested number of strips.

ViewTransition/PRPViewTransition.m
```
+ (PRPViewTransition *) viewWithView:(UIView *)view splitInto:(int)parts {
    PRPViewTransition *tempView = [[PRPViewTransition alloc]
                                        initWithFrame:view.frame];
    tempView.numLayers = parts;
    [tempView cutLayersFromImage:[view PRPCompositeView]];

    return [tempView autorelease];
}
```

The transition view initially acts as a static copy of the original view that it replaces and needs to be at the front of the main view hierarchy. When the MainViewController adds it to the view, the didMoveToSuperview delegate method is called. At this point we can start the transition process by creating the rotating tube of layers and then starting the switching animation process.

ViewTransition/PRPViewTransition.m
```
- (void)didMoveToSuperview {
    [self createRotatingLayers];
    [self SwitchLayers];
}
```

The numLayers property directly affects the size of the strips we create, and the transition effect can be made to look quite different by specifying different values. A high number creates quite narrow strips, resulting in a slower, tighter rotating tube; conversely, a low number creates wider strips that can result in the curl being too open and visually less effective.

The contentsRect property is the key to splitting up the image. We set the contents of each layer to contain the complete image, but by varying the contentsRect, we can constrain each subsequent strip to display only the portion of the image we want. By laying out each of the strips in a row, they appear identical to the original view. We use the parent layer here, stripLayer, only to contain our row of strips; it has no visible contents of its own.

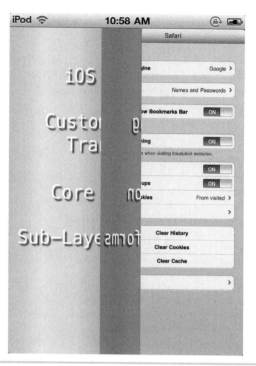

Figure 34—A partial page curl transition

ViewTransition/PRPViewTransition.m
```
- (void)cutLayersFromImage:(UIImage *)image {

    width = self.bounds.size.width/numLayers;
    height = self.bounds.size.height;
    unitSize = 1.0/numLayers;
    stripLayer = [CALayer layer];
    [self.layer addSublayer:stripLayer];
    for (int i = 0; i < numLayers; i++) {
        CALayer *layer = [CALayer layer];
        layer.contents = (id)image.CGImage;
        CGRect posRect = CGRectMake(width*i, 0, width, height);
        layer.contentsRect = CGRectMake(unitSize*i, 0, unitSize, 1);
        layer.frame = posRect;
        [stripLayer addSublayer:layer];
    }
}
```

The process involved in the createRotatingLayers method can be a little hard to picture but ultimately creates a multisided "tube" of transparent layers that are equal in size to the image strips we created earlier. The trick to building the tube is to add each of the "side" layers while gradually incrementing both the rotation and the translation transformation with a zPosition—the point around which the layer rotates, set to be equal to the radius of the tube cross section. To try to visualize this process in action, imagine building a tube out of identical strips of paper and adding each strip as a new side, rotated a little from the previous one, until we complete the circle.

Each of these tube layers is added to the transform layer, which then lets us use sublayer transformation to rotate the tube of layers as a single unit.

ViewTransition/PRPViewTransition.m
```objc
- (void) createRotatingLayers {
    transform = [CALayer layer];
    transform.frame = CGRectMake(self.bounds.size.width-width/2, 0, 1, 1);
    transform.backgroundColor = [UIColor whiteColor].CGColor;
    [self.layer addSublayer:transform];
    CATransform3D t = CATransform3DMakeTranslation(-width/2, 0, 0);
    for (int i=0; i < SIDES ; i++) {
        CALayer *rotLayer = [CALayer layer];
        rotLayer.anchorPoint = CGPointMake(1, 1);
        rotLayer.frame = CGRectMake(0, 0, width, height);
        rotLayer.zPosition = -width*0.866;
        rotLayer.transform = t;
        [transform addSublayer:rotLayer];

        t = CATransform3DRotate(t, -M_PI*2/SIDES, 0, 1, 0);
        t = CATransform3DTranslate(t, width, 0, 0);
    }
    count = 0;
    layerNum = 0;
}
```

There are two components to the animation of the transition, but both use sublayer transformation to animate the tube as a whole. The rotation animation and the translation animation are coordinated to effectively rotate the tube like a pencil rolling across the screen, but only to the point that the next side of the tube has rotated enough to be parallel with the view.

ViewTransition/PRPViewTransition.m
```objc
- (void) animateLayers {
    CABasicAnimation *anim = [CABasicAnimation
                    animationWithKeyPath:@"sublayerTransform.rotation.y"];
    anim.fromValue = [NSNumber numberWithFloat:-M_PI*2/SIDES*count];
    anim.toValue = [NSNumber numberWithFloat:-M_PI*2/SIDES*(count+1)];
    anim.duration = duration/numLayers;
    anim.removedOnCompletion = NO;
    anim.fillMode = kCAFillModeBoth;
    anim.delegate = self;
    [transform addAnimation:anim forKey:@"subRot"];
```

```
anim = [CABasicAnimation
            animationWithKeyPath:@"sublayerTransform.translation.x"];
anim.fromValue = [NSNumber numberWithFloat:-width*count];
anim.toValue = [NSNumber numberWithFloat:-width*(count+1)];
anim.duration = duration/numLayers*0.98;
anim.removedOnCompletion = NO;
anim.fillMode = kCAFillModeBoth;
[transform addAnimation:anim forKey:@"subTrans"];
count++;
}
```

The SwitchLayers method coupled with the animationDidStop delegate is the heart of the curl, or roll, effect. At each turn of the tube we swap the contents (strip of the original image) of the stripLayer with the layer of the tube now laying over it, almost as if it were now glued on. We then remove that strip from the stripLayer, and on the next rotation that layer appears to curl up toward us, as if peeling away from the backing view.

ViewTransition/PRPViewTransition.m
```
- (void) SwitchLayers {
    CALayer *oldLayer = [stripLayer.sublayers objectAtIndex:
                                    numLayers-count-1];
    CALayer * tLayer = [transform.sublayers objectAtIndex:layerNum];
    [CATransaction setValue:(id)kCFBooleanTrue
                    forKey:kCATransactionDisableActions];
    tLayer.contents = oldLayer.contents;
    [oldLayer removeFromSuperlayer];
    tLayer.contentsRect = CGRectMake(unitSize*(numLayers-count-1),
                                    0, unitSize, 1);
    [self animateLayers];
    layerNum--;
    if (layerNum < 0) layerNum = SIDES-1;
}
```

The animationDidStop delegate controls the sequence of turns of the tube, because it gradually "picks" up the layers of the backing image. At the end of the loop, we add an additional turn of the tube to make sure it is off the screen and then remove the tube from the view—its task complete.

ViewTransition/PRPViewTransition.m
```
- (void)animationDidStop:(CAAnimation *)theAnimation finished:(BOOL)flag {
    if (count < numLayers) {
        [self SwitchLayers];
    } else if (count == numLayers) {
        [self animateLayers];
    } else {  // Reached the end
        [self removeFromSuperview];
    }
}
```

To give the sample app a feel similar to a book-reading app, we use a UISwipeGestureRecognizer to trigger the transition, alternating between three sample images. All the hard work is done in the PRPViewTransition class, so the setup to implement it is quite simple. We create an instance of the class specifying the view to be transitioned and the number of images splits. We then set the duration of the transition and add it as a subview of the ViewController. Because the initializer of the transView has already made a copy of the original view, split into layers, we can now remove the original view from the viewController. The process of adding the view calls the didMoveToSuperview delegate and kicks off the transition animation.

ViewTransition/MainViewController.m

```objc
- (void)swiped:(UISwipeGestureRecognizer *)sender {
    NSString *splashImage;
    loop++;
    switch (loop) {
        case 1:
            splashImage = @"settings.png";
            break;
        case 2:
            splashImage = @"BackImage.jpg";
            break;
        default:
            splashImage = @"Default.png";
            loop = 0;
            break;
    }
    UIImageView *newView = [[UIImageView alloc] initWithImage:
                                    [UIImage imageNamed:splashImage]];
    newView.userInteractionEnabled = YES;
    newView.frame = self.view.bounds;
    [self.view addSubview:newView];
    PRPViewTransition *transView = [PRPViewTransition
                                    viewWithView:self.currentView
                                    splitInto:4];
    transView.duration = 0.8;
    [self.view addSubview:transView];
    [self.currentView removeFromSuperview];
    self.currentView = newView;
    [newView release];
}
```

The final transition is a reasonable simulation of a page turn, though by adjusting the number of slices it's also possible to create an effect closer to rolling the page away from the view. Currently the sample app works only in a single direction, but it shouldn't be too difficult to implement the reverse of the process—to curl a page back over the current view.

CHAPTER 4

Networking Recipes

A great number of mobile apps rely on web services for their core experience. The iOS SDK gives you the tools to connect to just about any type of service you need but at a relatively low level. There are plenty of standard interactions and operations that every networked app needs to make, and many of them require more code than you might expect.

The recipes in this section illustrate some reusable solutions for a few of these common situations. They're ready to use as is and easily extended to either go further or address your own requirements more directly.

Recipe 31

Tame the Network Activity Indicator

Problem

Your application performs downloads and uploads in multiple places, queuing or parallelizing them under heavy user activity. You need to reliably display network status without actively tracking every network operation.

Solution

We can use the networkActivityIndicatorVisible property on UIApplication to conveniently show and hide the network "spinner" in the status bar. This binary switch has no context, however. If we write an application that performs concurrent uploads and downloads, it quickly becomes hard to accurately report ongoing activity. Showing the indicator when every transaction starts is easy, but how do we know when to hide it? Whether we're using NSURLConnection or NSStream, our networking code should not necessarily be responsible for maintaining the context required to manage the network activity indicator. We'll solve this problem with a category on UIApplication that tracks network connections, automatically showing the indicator when activity begins and hiding it when it is finished. By using a category, we can call the existing UIApplication instance rather than managing another object. This especially makes sense since the activity indicator itself is managed by UIApplication.

This PRPNetworkActivity category maintains a read-only count of active connections. Two methods, -prp_pushNetworkActivity and -prp_popNetworkActivity, allow any code to notify the application of network activity. A -prp_resetNetworkActivity method clears the current state and starts from scratch.

NetworkActivityCenter/Classes/UIApplication+PRPNetworkActivity.h

```objc
@interface UIApplication (PRPNetworkActivity)

@property (nonatomic, assign, readonly) NSInteger prp_networkActivityCount;

- (void)prp_pushNetworkActivity;
- (void)prp_popNetworkActivity;
- (void)prp_resetNetworkActivity;

@end
```

Remember that because this is a category, it's important to prefix all of the method names to ensure they don't conflict with any methods Apple adds to UIApplication in future SDK releases.

The implementation is very simple: we declare a static prp_networkActivityCount variable, which the -prp_pushNetworkActivity and -prp_popNetworkActivity methods respectively increment and decrement. A simple getter method exposes the count in a read-only fashion.

NetworkActivityCenter/Classes/UIApplication+PRPNetworkActivity.m

```
- (NSInteger)prp_networkActivityCount {
    @synchronized(self) {
        return prp_networkActivityCount;
    }
}

- (void)prp_pushNetworkActivity {
    @synchronized(self) {
        prp_networkActivityCount++;
    }
    [self prp_refreshNetworkActivityIndicator];
}

- (void)prp_popNetworkActivity {
    @synchronized(self) {
        if (prp_networkActivityCount > 0) {
            prp_networkActivityCount--;
        } else {
            prp_networkActivityCount = 0;
            NSLog(@"%s Unbalanced network activity: count already 0.",
                    __PRETTY_FUNCTION__);
        }
    }
    [self prp_refreshNetworkActivityIndicator];
}
```

A few notes about this approach:

- We use a global to store the activity count, but our category methods operate on an instance of UIApplication. Always be careful when sharing statics between object instances. An ideal solution might use the associated object approach explained in Recipe 40, *Store Data in a Category*, on page 197, but since there is only a single UIApplication instance in a given app, we stuck with the global in the interest of simplicity.

- The methods listed earlier access the activity count while synchronizing on self, which is the shared application instance since we've written a category on UIApplication. We have added this synchronization because networking code that uses these category methods is likely to run on multiple threads. There is more than one way to synchronize Objective-C code, so we've chosen what we saw as the clearest solution.

The -prp_refreshNetworkActivityIndicator method sets the standard networkActivityIndicatorVisible property on UIApplication according to the current activity count: if the count is positive, the network activity indicator is shown; when it goes back down to 0, the indicator is hidden. Because most of the UIKit is not understood to be thread-safe and the networkActivityIndicatorVisible property is not explicitly documented as such, we write a check to ensure the network activity indicator is touched only from the main thread.

NetworkActivityCenter/Classes/UIApplication+PRPNetworkActivity.m
```
- (void)prp_refreshNetworkActivityIndicator {
    if (![NSThread isMainThread]) {
        SEL sel_refresh = @selector(prp_refreshNetworkActivityIndicator);
        [self performSelectorOnMainThread:sel_refresh
                               withObject:nil
                            waitUntilDone:NO];
        return;
    }

    BOOL active = (self.prp_networkActivityCount > 0);
    self.networkActivityIndicatorVisible = active;
}
```

We now have reliable network state management accessible from anywhere in our application and completely decoupled from the rest of our code. Just call -prp_pushNetworkActivity whenever starting a connection, and call -prp_popNetworkActivity whenever the connection terminates.

The NetworkActivityCenter sample project demonstrates this code in action. We've modified the PRPDownload class from an earlier recipe to push and pop activity based on the status of each download. Neither these download objects nor the test app's view controller has any idea of one another, let alone what each is doing with the network. Each object reports its state to the UIApplication category methods, which decide when the network activity indicator should be activated or deactivated.

This project illustrates an application of the asynchronous PRPConnection mechanism from Recipe 32, *Simplify Web Service Connections*, on page 153. We've tied a download to each row in the table and modified the PRPConnection class to use the category methods from this recipe. The network activity indicator shows as soon as downloads begin and automatically hides when the last download is finished or interrupted. The code you see in this class stays the same whether 1 or 100 downloads are in progress.

Recipe 32

Simplify Web Service Connections

Problem

You want to download data from a web service with minimal code and complexity. Where do you start?

Solution

The NSURLConnection class included with the iPhone SDK provides a clean, flexible interface for downloading web-based data of any type or size. It also requires a lot of repetitive setup code everywhere we intend to use it. Most of the time, we just want to kick off a download in the background and get our file or data back when it's completed.

We can minimize the work necessary for each download and save ourselves a lot of repetition by wrapping a simpler interface around NSURLConnection. This class, PRPConnection, manages the temporary data structure and tracks progress that our own controller object would normally be responsible for so that the calling code needs to respond only when the download is complete and the data is ready. We'll also create an optional hook for monitoring download progress.

The class contains an NSURLConnection object (of course), as well as numerous other pieces of information not provided by NSURLConnection:

- Destination URL

- Originating NSURLRequest

- Expected download size

- Download completion (percent) to date

```
SimpleDownload/Classes/PRPConnection.h
@property (nonatomic, copy, readonly) NSURL *url;
@property (nonatomic, copy, readonly) NSURLRequest *urlRequest;
@property (nonatomic, assign, readonly) NSInteger contentLength;
@property (nonatomic, retain, readonly) NSMutableData *downloadData;
@property (nonatomic, assign, readonly) float percentComplete;
@property (nonatomic, assign) NSUInteger progressThreshold;
```

We create the connection by simply passing the destination URL and optional Objective-C blocks for handling connection progress, completion, or failure. A convenience method for passing your own NSURLRequest is also there, which will come in handy once we discuss HTTP POST uploads in the next two chapters.

SimpleDownload/Classes/PRPConnection.h
```
+ (id)connectionWithURL:(NSURL *)requestURL
        progressBlock:(PRPConnectionProgressBlock)progress
      completionBlock:(PRPConnectionCompletionBlock)completion;

+ (id)connectionWithRequest:(NSURLRequest *)request
          progressBlock:(PRPConnectionProgressBlock)progress
        completionBlock:(PRPConnectionCompletionBlock)completion;
```

Unlike NSURLConnection, we don't start the connections immediately. This is so we can further configure the connection before proceeding, as you'll see momentarily. Explicit -start and -stop methods are provided to explicitly begin or cancel the connection.

So let's take a closer look at the blocks. We've defined two: one for reporting incremental progress and another for reporting completion or failure. The completion block's error parameter is passed on from the NSURLConnection delegate method -connection:didFailWithError:. If the connection finished successfully, the error is nil.

SimpleDownload/Classes/PRPConnection.h
```
typedef void (^PRPConnectionProgressBlock)(PRPConnection *connection);
typedef void (^PRPConnectionCompletionBlock)(PRPConnection *connection,
                                             NSError *error);
```

Since PRPConnection is a wrapper around NSURLConnection, it acts as the NSURL-Connection's delegate, saving data incrementally as the download progresses. As this happens, the progress block is invoked for every 1 percent change in progress. You can customize this frequency by setting the progressThreshold property. A value of 5, for example, means the block is invoked for every 5 percent change in progress. This allows you to easily present PRPConnection progress in a number of different ways. If you don't care about progress, just pass a nil progress block when creating the connection.

The contentLength property represents the Content-Length value in the response header of the connection. This value is set when we receive the standard -connection:didReceiveResponse: NSURLConnection delegate method.

SimpleDownload/Classes/PRPConnection.m
```
- (void)connection:(NSURLConnection *)connection
didReceiveResponse:(NSURLResponse *)response {
```

Working with NSError

Our completion block checks the passed NSError parameter for nil in order to determine success. This is safe because the error is a known quantity; it is only non-nil when received in -connection:didFailWithError:, an explicit error condition.

This is very different from passing an NSError object by reference to an Apple API such as -[NSManagedObjectContext executeFetchRequest:error:]. In those cases, you must check the return value before inspecting the NSError object, as explained in the reference documentation for the API in question.

```objc
if ([response isKindOfClass:[NSHTTPURLResponse class]]) {
    NSHTTPURLResponse *httpResponse = (NSHTTPURLResponse *)response;
    if ([httpResponse statusCode] == 200) {
        NSDictionary *header = [httpResponse allHeaderFields];
        NSString *contentLen = [header valueForKey:@"Content-Length"];
        NSInteger length = self.contentLength = [contentLen integerValue];
        self.downloadData = [NSMutableData dataWithCapacity:length];
    }
}
}
```

We use this value, along with the latest size of the downloaded data, to compute the percentComplete property.

SimpleDownload/Classes/PRPConnection.m
```objc
- (float)percentComplete {
    if (self.contentLength <= 0) return 0;
    return (([self.downloadData length] * 1.0f) / self.contentLength) * 100;
}
```

We invoke the progress block whenever percentComplete reaches a multiple of the specified threshold.

SimpleDownload/Classes/PRPConnection.m
```objc
- (void)connection:(NSURLConnection *)connection
    didReceiveData:(NSData *)data {
    [self.downloadData appendData:data];
    float pctComplete = floor([self percentComplete]);
    if ((pctComplete - self.previousMilestone) >= self.progressThreshold) {
        self.previousMilestone = pctComplete;
        if (self.progressBlock) self.progressBlock(self);
    }
}
```

Using PRPConnection is easy: create one by calling +downloadWithURL:progress-Block:completionBlock:, and then call -start. PRPConnection takes care of all the heavy lifting, leaving us to handle only the events we care about. When the download is finished, just access the downloadData property. You can also check the length of the downloadData's bytes array if you want to display that information to the user as the download progresses.

Explore the SimpleDownloadViewController class implementation provided with the SimpleDownloads test project, and note how few lines of code are needed to handle the actual download: nearly all the work is limited to manipulation of the user interface. This abstraction of NSURLConnection allows us to keep our controller code clean and focused on its important, higher-level tasks. We can use it to acquire RSS feeds, get JSON responses from web services, and even download media.

Note that for large downloads, you'll want to wire this up to an NSInputStream and write the data to disk as it comes down in order to avoid memory pressure. Downloading a 500MB video directly to an NSData object in memory, for example, will inevitably crash your app.

Recipe 33

Format a Simple HTTP POST

Problem

New web service APIs pop up every day. Sooner or later one of them will require an HTTP POST instead of a plain old GET. How do you format such a request? How do you make it easy for every project that needs it?

Solution

If you've used (or coded for) the Web, you're no stranger to POST methods. When filling out a form on a web page with basic drop-downs and text fields, followed by some kind of "submit" action, that form probably produces a "form" or "URL encoded" POST. On the Web, however, the browser does the dirty work. What's a Cocoa programmer to do?

The good news is we can do a POST with the same NSURLConnection API we've used for other more basic web requests (usually GET methods). Submitting a POST involves a few simple additions:

- Setting the request method to POST

- Identifying the type of POST we're submitting

- Adding form data to the request body

The connection itself is unchanged; it's the supporting NSURLRequest that needs modification. To do this, we'll write a subclass of NSMutableURLRequest, PRPFormEncodedPOSTRequest, which supports a dictionary of parameters to be used in the POST method. We subclass NSMutableURLRequest so we can add the form data to the HTTP body.

BasicHTTPPost/PRPFormEncodedPOSTRequest.h

```objc
@interface PRPFormEncodedPOSTRequest : NSMutableURLRequest {}

+ (id)requestWithURL:(NSURL *)url formParameters:(NSDictionary *)params;
- (id)initWithURL:(NSURL *)url formParameters:(NSDictionary *)params;

- (void)setFormParameters:(NSDictionary *)params;

@end
```

The first two steps outlined earlier are simple: set the HTTP method to POST, and set the content type to application/x-www-form-urlencoded. We can do this work at initialization time.

BasicHTTPPost/PRPFormEncodedPOSTRequest.m

```
- (id)initWithURL:(NSURL *)url formParameters:(NSDictionary *)params {
    if ((self = [super initWithURL:url])) {
        [self setHTTPMethod:@"POST"];
        [self setValue:@"application/x-www-form-urlencoded"
    forHTTPHeaderField:@"Content-Type"];
        [self setFormParameters:params];
    }
    return self;
}
```

That -setFormParameters: method is the remaining piece of the puzzle. In the case of our -initWithURL:formParameters: method, the parameters are passed at creation time, but we could also set them after creating the object, so it's broken out into a separate method.

Form parameters look a lot like a URL query string, but instead of being appended to the URL, they're placed in the HTTP body. So, if we are submitting a form that includes your name and age, the composed body string might look like this:

name=Lucas+Drance&age=1.5

Each parameter's name and value are connected with an equal sign (=), and the pairs are connected with an ampersand (&). In this recipe, we use %20 to escape spaces, rather than the plus (+) characters specified by RFC 2616. In practice, many servers accept either, but unfortunately many popular web services don't support the plus sign. Always test your project with whitespace content to make sure the server you're talking to is behaving as expected.

So, given a set of name-value pairs, our Cocoa code needs to tie them together, as explained earlier. This is what -setFormParameters: does for us. An NSString category handles any necessary escaping.

BasicHTTPPost/PRPFormEncodedPOSTRequest.m

```
- (void)setFormParameters:(NSDictionary *)params {
    NSStringEncoding enc = NSUTF8StringEncoding;
    NSMutableString *postBody = [NSMutableString string];
    for (NSString *paramKey in params) {
        if ([paramKey length] > 0) {
            NSString *value = [params objectForKey:paramKey];
            NSString *encodedValue =
                [value prp_URLEncodedFormStringUsingEncoding:enc];
```

```
            NSUInteger length = [postBody length];
            NSString *paramFormat = (length == 0 ? @"%@=%@" : @"&%@=%@");
            [postBody appendFormat:paramFormat, paramKey, encodedValue];
        }
    }
    NSLog(@"postBody is now %@", postBody);
    [self setHTTPBody:[postBody dataUsingEncoding:enc]];
}
```

Simple, right? Actually, we need to do a bit more work to account for reserved characters.

The standard -[NSString stringByAddingPercentEscapesUsingEncoding:] method claims to "convert the receiver into a legal URL string." This sounds promising, but we need more than that. What happens if the actual user input contains one of our reserved characters (+, &, =)? Nothing. These characters are technically "legal," so NSString leaves them alone. However, a server might mistake a user-entered + for a space. Worse, user-entered ampersands will prematurely signal a new parameter. So although these characters are legal, they are not safe for our use. We need to escape them manually, and that's where our category methods come in.

Our first category method, -prp_URLEncodedFormStringUsingEncoding:, is used by our request class to construct the HTTP body. It escapes the aforementioned reserved characters and then replaces each space with a plus (+). Order is important here: if we replace the spaces first, then our escape procedure will escape all of our pluses. We want only the user-entered pluses escaped, so we replace the spaces last.

BasicHTTPPost/NSString+PRPURLAdditions.m
```
- (NSString *)prp_URLEncodedFormStringUsingEncoding:(NSStringEncoding)enc {
    NSString *escapedStringWithSpaces =
    [self prp_percentEscapedStringWithEncoding:enc
                                   additionalCharacters:@"&=+"
                                     ignoredCharacters:nil];
    return escapedStringWithSpaces;
}
```

The string conversion is done by our second category method, -prp_URLEncodedFormStringUsingEncoding:additionalCharacters:ignoredCharacters:. It takes two sets of characters: those that should be escaped (the reserved characters) and those that shouldn't (the spaces—at least not right away). We've already determined that NSString can't solve our problems, so we need to head down beneath Cocoa to its C counterpart, Core Foundation. A call to CFURLCreateStringByAddingPercentEscapes performs the specialized substitution we need, using our additionalCharacters and ignoredCharacters for custom behavior.

BasicHTTPPost/NSString+PRPURLAdditions.m

```
- (NSString *)prp_percentEscapedStringWithEncoding:(NSStringEncoding)enc
                             additionalCharacters:(NSString *)add
                               ignoredCharacters:(NSString *)ignore {
    CFStringEncoding convertedEncoding =
        CFStringConvertNSStringEncodingToEncoding(enc);
    return [(NSString *)CFURLCreateStringByAddingPercentEscapes(
                                            kCFAllocatorDefault,
                                            (CFStringRef)self,
                                            (CFStringRef)ignore,
                                            (CFStringRef)add,
                                            convertedEncoding)
            autorelease];
}
```

Let's review what's going on here. The built-in behavior of Core Foundation (and thus Cocoa) is to escape only characters that are fundamentally illegal for use in URLs. Our POST use case, however, requires that some technically legal characters still be escaped. We accomplish that by passing &=+ for additionalCharacters.

Finally: a well-formed POST body string! Now we just get the data as UTF-8 (or whatever encoding your server requires) and set it as the request body. With the request in place, all we need to do now is create an NSURLConnection with our special request and submit it.

BasicHTTPPost/PRPURLEncodedPostViewController.m

```
NSURL *postURL = [NSURL URLWithString:URLString];
NSURLRequest *postRequest;
postRequest = [PRPFormEncodedPOSTRequest requestWithURL:postURL
                                        formParameters:params];

NSURLResponse *response = nil;
NSError *error = nil;
NSData *responseData = [NSURLConnection sendSynchronousRequest:postRequest
                                          returningResponse:&response
                                                     error:&error];
```

Now you just need to test all this work. The BasicHTTPPost project includes a simple WEBrick servlet[1] that will receive POST methods and echo the output back. To run it, just navigate to the directory containing webserver.rb and type ruby webserver.rb. You should see some output indicating the server has started. To verify the server is running, drag the local form.html file into a browser, fill out the form, submit it, and check the response. Once you've verified the static HTML form works, run BasicHTTPPost and see what happens when you enter the same information into the iPhone app.

---

1. Special thanks to Mike Clark for contributing this recipe's test server code.

Work asynchronously!

The BasicHTTPPost project accompanying this chapter uses a synchronous connection to demonstrate the POST. This is merely to demonstrate the solution with as few lines as possible, since the focus is on building the request itself. Apple strongly recommends using NSURLConnection in asynchronous mode.

So there you have it...a straightforward and reusable mechanism for building form-based POST requests on demand.

Recipe 34

Upload Files Over HTTP

Problem

In the previous chapter, we discussed submitting form data in an HTTP POST using NSURLConnection and a custom NSMutableURLRequest subclass that hosted the HTTP body. With file/photo/video sharing on the rise, however, simple forms won't always cut it. So, how do we upload a file to a website from Cocoa?

Solution

If we adopt a web API that accepts files, we're almost certainly going to be asked to perform a multipart POST. This still involves setting data (lots of it being text) to the HTTP body, but it is much more complicated than posting a simple URL-encoded body string.

As RFC 1867[2] and RFC 1341[3] explain, a multipart body involves a combination of traditional form fields and binary file data, separated by an arbitrary "boundary" string. Here's what a multipart body for a username, password, and JPEG upload might look like:

```
--d0ntcr055t3h57r33m2
Content-Disposition: form-data; name="username"

tyler
--d0ntcr055t3h57r33m2
Content-Disposition: form-data; name="password"

durden
--d0ntcr055t3h57r33m2
Content-Disposition: form-data; name="media"; filename="foo.jpg"
Content-Type: image/jpeg

<data from foo.jpg>
--d0ntcr055t3h57r33m2
```

---

2. http://tools.ietf.org/html/rfc1867

3. http://www.w3.org/Protocols/rfc1341/7_2_Multipart.html

We've cut out the actual JPEG data, but as you can imagine, it's quite noisy. This giant string is our HTTP body. The boundary string, d0ntcr055t3h57r33m2, is defined in the request header. Formatting this body with the boundary, the content-disposition headers, the line breaks, and the data itself is our responsibility. This can get very messy very quickly, and one wrong piece can spoil the entire upload.

Our goal is to add some sanity to this process so we don't have to reinvent the wheel every time we're ready to upload a file.

Once again, we declare a subclass of NSMutableURLRequest—this time called PRPMultipartPOSTRequest. The class declares a dictionary for traditional key-value form parameters, which you can configure as you need. There's also an HTTP boundary property for use in the POST body. You should always set a fairly unique boundary when performing a multipart upload.

MultipartHTTPPost/PRPMultipartPOSTRequest.h
```
@property (nonatomic, copy) NSString *HTTPBoundary;
@property (nonatomic, retain) NSDictionary *formParameters;
```

Next, we have a method for setting the file to upload. It requires a content type, a form variable name, and a destination filename on the server.

MultipartHTTPPost/PRPMultipartPOSTRequest.h
```
- (void)setUploadFile:(NSString *)path
          contentType:(NSString *)type
            nameParam:(NSString *)nameParam
             filename:(NSString *)fileName;
```

Finally, there's a method to prepare the HTTP body for upload. It takes two blocks: one for successful completion and the other for any error that occurred while constructing the body. We'll explain why these blocks are necessary (as opposed to a simple return value) shortly.

MultipartHTTPPost/PRPMultipartPOSTRequest.h
```
- (void)prepareForUploadWithCompletionBlock:(PRPBodyCompletionBlock)completion
                                 errorBlock:(PRPBodyErrorBlock)error;
```

The complete flow for using PRPMultipartPOSTRequest is as follows:

1. Create a request object.

2. Set a custom boundary.

3. Set basic form parameters (if needed).

4. Add an upload file.

5. Prepare the request for submission.

Uploading Multiple Files

This chapter covers uploading a single file with a multipart/form-data content type. Other servers and APIs may require a combination of multipart/form-data and multipart/mixed data. Between the examples in RFC 1867 and ideally the server's documented requirements, it should be easy to extend this code to fit your needs.

The file and parameter steps are interchangeable. As we saw in the earlier example, any basic form data is presented as "Content-Disposition: form-data;" with the parameter name, followed by two line breaks and the value. The binary data for the file attachment is similarly structured in the body but also includes a content type and the aforementioned filename.

So, we have all the pieces we need; now we just have to glue it all together. This is where -prepareForUploadWithCompletionBlock:errorBlock: comes in: it takes any previously set parameters and the upload file and prepares a full multipart body from them.

We start by identifying the HTTP body as a multipart POST. We also set a temporary filename for the body content itself. Since this body is more complicated, and potentially much larger, than our basic POST, saving the body to a file makes it easier to recover from errors, interruptions, or app termination. It also prevents us from potentially running out of memory by managing all of this data in memory.

MultipartHTTPPost/PRPMultipartPOSTRequest.m
```objc
- (void)startRequestBody {
    if (!self.started) {
        self.started = YES;

        [self setHTTPMethod:@"POST"];
        NSString *format = @"multipart/form-data; boundary=%@";
        NSString *contentType = [NSString stringWithFormat:format,
                                 self.HTTPBoundary];
        [self setValue:contentType forHTTPHeaderField:@"Content-Type"];

        CFUUIDRef uuid = CFUUIDCreate(kCFAllocatorDefault);
        CFStringRef uuidStr = CFUUIDCreateString(kCFAllocatorDefault, uuid);
        NSString *extension = @"multipartbody";
        NSString *bodyFileName = [(NSString *)uuidStr
                                  stringByAppendingPathExtension:extension];
        CFRelease(uuidStr);
        CFRelease(uuid);

        self.pathToBodyFile = [NSTemporaryDirectory()
                               stringByAppendingPathComponent:bodyFileName];
```

Managing Temporary Files

This recipe saves the body to the temp directory with a randomized filename. The system cleans out the temp directory automatically at unspecified intervals, so if you want to manage the files yourself, save them to caches, documents, or some other directory in your app's sandbox. Remember, though, that you will then be responsible for deleting the body file when it's no longer neeeded.

```
        NSString *bodyPath = self.pathToBodyFile;
        self.bodyFileOutputStream = [NSOutputStream
                                  outputStreamToFileAtPath:bodyPath
                                                    append:YES];

        [self.bodyFileOutputStream open];
    }
}
```

The form parameters are prepared in a similar fashion to what we did for Recipe 33, *Format a Simple HTTP POST*, on page 157, except we don't need to escape the values. Following the pattern in the sample body shown earlier, each parameter is preceded by the HTTP boundary and a Content-Disposition identifier. We build all the parameters as a single string that's written out to the body as UTF-8 bytes. The UTF-8 conversion is done in the -appendBodyString: method.

MultipartHTTPPost/PRPMultipartPOSTRequest.m
```
NSMutableString *params = [NSMutableString string];
NSArray *keys = [self.formParameters allKeys];
for (NSString *key in keys) {
    NSAutoreleasePool *pool = [[NSAutoreleasePool alloc] init];
    [params appendString:[self preparedBoundary]];
    NSString *fmt = @"Content-Disposition: form-data; name=\"%@\"\r\n\r\n";
    [params appendFormat:fmt, key];
    [params appendFormat:@"%@", [self.formParameters objectForKey:key]];
    [pool release];
}
if ([params length]) {
    if ([self appendBodyString:params] == -1) {
        self.prepErrorBlock(self, [self.bodyFileOutputStream streamError]);
        return;
    }
}
```

Next up is the media file we're uploading. Easily handled: just append its data to the working body, right? Wrong! What if the file is a 10MB image or a 100MB movie? We can't just load that into memory as an NSData object—we're sure to run out of memory and crash. But we need to merge this file data into our HTTP body somehow. We'll accomplish that by using an input stream. An input stream operates on a run loop and allows us to incrementally load segments of data so we avoid exhausting resources. By setting ourselves as the input stream's delegate, we can find out when it is ready to read more data. It's a very similar flow to the asynchronous mode of NSURLConnection.

MultipartHTTPPost/PRPMultipartPOSTRequest.m

```
if (self.fileToUpload) {
    NSMutableString *str = [[NSMutableString alloc] init];
    [str appendString:[self preparedBoundary]];
    [str appendString:@"Content-Disposition: form-data; "];
    [str appendFormat:@"name=\"%@\"; ", self.fileToUpload.nameParam];
    [str appendFormat:@"filename=\"%@\"\r\n", self.fileToUpload.fileName];
    NSString *contentType = self.fileToUpload.contentType;
    [str appendFormat:@"Content-Type: %@\r\n\r\n", contentType];
    [self appendBodyString:str];

    NSLog(@"Preparing to stream %@", self.fileToUpload.localPath);
    NSString *path = self.fileToUpload.localPath;
    NSInputStream *mediaInputStream = [[NSInputStream alloc]
                                    initWithFileAtPath:path];
    self.uploadFileInputStream = mediaInputStream;
    [mediaInputStream release];

    [self.uploadFileInputStream setDelegate:self];
    [self.uploadFileInputStream scheduleInRunLoop:[NSRunLoop currentRunLoop]
                                    forMode:NSDefaultRunLoopMode];
    [self.uploadFileInputStream open];
} else {
    [self handleStreamCompletion];
}
```

The media is piped into our body file by the -stream:handleEvent: delegate method. We'll receive this message indefinitely as long as the stream has more data to read; when we do, we just take that data and send it right to our body file. When the input stream reaches the end, we finalize the body by calling -handleStreamCompletion.

MultipartHTTPPost/PRPMultipartPOSTRequest.m

```
case NSStreamEventHasBytesAvailable:
    len = [self.uploadFileInputStream read:buf maxLength:1024];
    if (len) {
        [self.bodyFileOutputStream write:buf maxLength:len];
    } else {
        NSLog(@"Buffer finished; wrote to %@", self.pathToBodyFile);
        [self handleStreamCompletion];
    }
    break;
```

Memory Management

The stream code you see in this recipe might seem like overkill for simple image uploads. However, it works perfectly fine and more importantly works exactly the same for extremely large files.

Run the MultipartHTTPPOST project under the Activity Monitor instrument to see how much memory is consumed with the supplied JPEG file. Then add a large file (for example, a 50MB movie). You should see little to no change in the app's memory consumption at runtime, despite a much larger upload. This is the power of streams, and it's invaluable on a platform like iOS.

The input stream's asynchronous behavior is why we use blocks to notify the caller of completion or errors: unlike the basic POST recipe, preparing this HTTP body is not a synchronous operation. The caller needs to wait over multiple run loop iterations for the input stream to finish its job.

At the end of the process, we tear down the media input stream and then write one last HTTP boundary to the body file. Remember, this body file is even larger than the media we just streamed, so it may not be safe to load this into memory either. Rather than set body data as we did for the basic POST recipe, we set an input stream to the body file we've created. When everything is done, we invoke the completion block that was passed on to -prepareForUploadWithCompletionBlock:errorBlock:.

MultipartHTTPPost/PRPMultipartPOSTRequest.m
```
- (void)handleStreamCompletion {
    [self finishMediaInputStream];
    [self finishRequestBody];
    self.prepCompletionBlock(self);
}

- (void)finishMediaInputStream {
    [self.uploadFileInputStream close];
    [self.uploadFileInputStream removeFromRunLoop:[NSRunLoop currentRunLoop]
                                          forMode:NSDefaultRunLoopMode];
    self.uploadFileInputStream = nil;
}
```

Our multipart POST request is now complete. The calling code then creates an NSURLConnection using the prepared request and awaits news of completion. The MultipartHTTPPost project reviews how this whole process works from start to finish.

MultipartHTTPPost/iPhone/AppDelegate_iPhone.m

```objc
- (void)upload:(id)sender {
    NSString *URLString = @"http://localhost:3000/upload";
    self.request = [PRPMultipartPOSTRequest
                        requestWithURL:[NSURL URLWithString:URLString]];
    self.request.HTTPBoundary = @"d0ntcr055t3h57r33m2";
    NSMutableDictionary *params;
    params = [NSMutableDictionary dictionaryWithObjectsAndKeys:
                @"Tyler", @"name",
                @"Soap salesman", @"occupation",
                nil];
    self.request.formParameters = params;

    NSString *imgFile = [[NSBundle mainBundle]
                        pathForResource:@"pic" ofType:@"jpg"];
    [self.request setUploadFile:imgFile
                    contentType:@"image/jpeg"
                      nameParam:@"filedata"
                       filename:@"uploadedPic.jpg"];

    PRPBodyCompletionBlock completionBlock;
    completionBlock = ^(PRPMultipartPOSTRequest *req) {
        NSLog(@"Completion Block!");
        NSURLResponse *response = nil;
        NSError *error = nil;
        NSData *responseData;
        responseData = [NSURLConnection sendSynchronousRequest:request
                                              returningResponse:&response
                                                          error:&error];
        if ([responseData length] > 0) {
            NSLog(@"Upload response: %@",
                [NSString stringWithCString:[responseData bytes]
                                   encoding:NSUTF8StringEncoding]);
        } else {
            NSLog(@"Bad response (%@)", responseData);
        }
    };
    PRPBodyErrorBlock errBlk = ^(PRPMultipartPOSTRequest *req,
                                 NSError *error) {
        NSLog(@"ERROR BLOCK (%@)", error);
    };

    [self.request prepareForUploadWithCompletionBlock:completionBlock
                                           errorBlock:errBlk];
}
```

Like the basic POST recipe, this project includes a simple WEBrick servlet to test this code.[4] To run it, navigate to the directory containing webserver.rb

---

4. Special thanks to Mike Clark for contributing this recipe's test server code.

and type ruby webserver.rb. You should see some output indicating the server has started. To verify the server is running, drag the local form.html file into a browser, fill out the form, submit it, and check the response. Once you've verified the static HTML form works, move on to verify the MultipartHTTPPost project.

Between this recipe and the earlier basic POST recipe, you should be well prepared to support a variety of web service uploads.

CHAPTER 5

Runtime Recipes

These recipes cover a broad range of iOS topics including UIKit, Core Data, and the Objective-C runtime. They illustrate techniques that can help you gather information during an inevitable troubleshooting session and bring order to potentially chaotic areas of your project, or they introduce you to newer features of the Objective-C language that you may not be using. In all cases, the goal is to help you be a smarter, more efficient iOS developer.

Recipe 35

Leverage Modern Objective-C Class Design

Problem

Objective-C has a long history and an extremely deep set of frameworks. The language's traditionally verbose nature can lead to noisy header files and implementations that are hard to read or maintain. How do you keep your interfaces clean and readable without compromising functionality?

Solution

Many of the recipes in this book take advantage of recent developments in Objective-C and Clang to keep the code lean and readable. It's worth discussing these techniques up front so you can understand their motivations and ideally find ways of using them to make your own projects easier to manage and maintain.

Let's start with a simple Cocoa class representing a book that defines some private, read-only data wrapped in properties. It's a contrived example but sufficient for the goals of this recipe.

ClassExtension/PRPBook.h
```
@interface PRPBook : NSObject {
@private
    NSString *title;
    NSArray *authors;
    BOOL inStock;
}

@property (nonatomic, copy, readonly) NSString *title;
@property (nonatomic, copy, readonly) NSArray *authors;

@property (nonatomic, assign, readonly, getter=isInStock) BOOL inStock;

@end
```

It's a shame that those private instance variables (*ivars*) are visible in the header for everyone to see. It's also redundant to have the properties *and* the ivars listed. Well, as of the iOS 4.0 SDK, we can eliminate this redundancy and just declare the properties: the tools and runtime synthesize the underlying ivar for us. This means that we can type less, have less to read, and, more importantly, not have private data in a public header.

Our new header file reads much better without the redundant ivar declarations, protects our ivars from external access, and gives our poor hands and wrists a break.

ClassExtension/PRPModernBook.h
```
@interface PRPModernBook : NSObject {}

@property (nonatomic, copy) NSString *title;
@property (nonatomic, copy) NSArray *authors;

@property (nonatomic, assign, readonly, getter=isInStock) BOOL inStock;

@end
```

Now let's look at the implementation. We of course synthesize our properties, and we also have an internal method for refreshing the book's in-stock or out-of-stock status. The calling code should never have to worry about refreshing the object, so we want to leave this method out of the header.

ClassExtension/PRPBook.m
```
- (id)init {
    if ((self = [super init])) {
        [self refreshStock];
    }
    return self;
}

- (void)refreshStock {
    // ...
}
```

When we build this code, the compiler throws a warning because -refreshStock is referenced in -init but defined below it. The compiler reads from the top down, so we can fix this problem either by declaring -refreshStock in the header or by moving it up above -init. Neither option is desirable, however, because we want it to be private—not displayed in the header. And we don't want the compiler dictating the structure of our code. So, how do we make both ourselves and the compiler happy?

The answer lies in private class extensions, a new feature of Objective-C 2.0. Class extensions are effectively private interfaces to the class you're writing, typically defined alongside your standard implementation. These extensions look very much like categories, but they are significantly different.

> ## Runtime Trivia
>
> The iOS device runtime has always been able to synthesize ivars; it's the iPhone Simulator runtime that required explicitly declared ivars. With the 4.0 SDK, the simulator has been brought up to speed, and we can omit ivar declarations where a property exists.

You define a private class extension by declaring an interface with the same name as your class, followed by empty parentheses. You then fill that interface with any methods you don't want in the header but need to formally declare for correctness.

```
@interface PRPModernBook ()

- (void)refreshStock;

@end
```

Again, this looks just like a category. But the big difference here is that this extension is treated as a formal component of the class. So, the compiler actually complains if it does not find matching implementations. (That's not so for categories.) This policy protects you at compile time from making potentially harmful omissions or typos.

The other big difference is that you can declare new storage (synthesized properties) in a class extension. Categories, by contrast, only support the addition of functionality (methods). So if we have a property that we want to use internally, and not expose in the header, we can now do that with a class extension. Combined with synthesized ivars, the private data is completely absent from the header.

```
@interface PRPModernBook ()

@property (nonatomic, retain) id privateContext;

- (void)refreshStock;

@end
```

It gets better. The inStock property is naturally defined in the header as read-only, since we don't want an arbitrary caller modifying that state. But wouldn't it be nice if internal code could use the property to set the state over time? Class extensions allow this too. So although the public property in the header is readonly:

```
@property (nonatomic, assign, readonly, getter=isInStock) BOOL inStock;
```

our class extension enables private readwrite access. Here, now, is the full private class extension for PRPModernBook:

```
ClassExtension/PRPModernBook.m
@interface PRPModernBook ()

@property (nonatomic, retain) id privateContext;
@property (nonatomic, assign, readwrite, getter=isInStock) BOOL inStock;

- (void)refreshStock;

@end
```

We've done a whole lot here: made a much clearer contract with whoever reads the headers, obscured private data and API from the reader, and given private callers enhanced property access over public callers. We've even reduced the amount of code we have to write!

The Objective-C 2.0 modern runtime and class extensions can help you write more readable, structured, and maintainable code. You'll see them used frequently in this book; we hide boring details and private features in class extensions (and eliminate redundant ivars altogether) so that the headers are very clear about how the class should be used. As a class gets larger over time, this technique only becomes more valuable.

Recipe 36

Produce Intelligent Debug Output

Problem

You litter your source with printf and NSLog statements during development and spend hours commenting them out when it's time to ship. Extraneous log statements hurt performance and can reduce the life span of a device's solid-state drive. You're looking for a way to simplify the process of removing this log output.

Solution

A good 90 percent of log output, maybe even more, exists only to aid us during the development process. Error reporting is still necessary in production code, but most of the log statements we write will eventually need to go away. Xcode makes it easy to support conditional logging based on a project's build configuration. With just a few lines of code and a single change to our target or scheme settings, we can have log statements that magically disappear for our Release and Distribution builds.

When it comes to basic logging, Cocoa's NSLog() function is handy, but it's both unconditional and not very customizable. Here we'll create a logging function that allows us to fine-tune the information logged with each call and also turn itself off when running in nondebug configurations.

We start by writing the new logging function, PRPDebug(). This function takes a format string with variable arguments, just like NSLog(). With every call, it additionally prints the following:

- Timestamp

- Process name

- Originating filename and line number

DebugOutput/Classes/PRPDebug.m
```
void PRPDebug(const char *fileName, int lineNumber, NSString *fmt, ...) {
    va_list args;
    va_start(args, fmt);
```

```objc
static NSDateFormatter *debugFormatter = nil;
if (debugFormatter == nil) {
    debugFormatter = [[NSDateFormatter alloc] init];
    [debugFormatter setDateFormat:@"yyyyMMdd.HH:mm:ss"];
}

NSString *msg = [[NSString alloc] initWithFormat:fmt arguments:args];
NSString *filePath = [[NSString alloc] initWithUTF8String:fileName];
NSString *timestamp = [debugFormatter stringFromDate:[NSDate date]];

NSDictionary *info = [[NSBundle mainBundle] infoDictionary];
NSString *appName = [info objectForKey:(NSString *)kCFBundleNameKey];
fprintf(stdout, "%s %s[%s:%d] %s\n",
        [timestamp UTF8String],
        [appName UTF8String],
        [[filePath lastPathComponent] UTF8String],
        lineNumber,
        [msg UTF8String]);

va_end(args);
[msg release];
[filePath release];
}
```

The timestamp and process name resemble information provided by NSLog, though formatted a bit differently so the two styles can be easily distinguished. The debugFormatter object is statically allocated because initializing an NSDateFormatter object is very expensive. If we created a new formatter with each call, heavy use of PRPDebug() could significantly affect our application's performance. iOS 4.0 introduces new class methods on NSDateFormatter that relieve us of this optimization burden, but since this recipe is particularly useful, we decided to keep it compatible with 3.0 and later.

The filename and line number are very valuable: they tell us exactly where in our code a particular log statement is coming from. We'll see how that information is generated in a moment.

So, we've written a function called PRPDebug. You may have noticed, however, that the code in DebugOutputAppDelegate calls PRPLog. What is PRPLog? It is, in fact, a macro. This is what we use to enable conditional execution of the log statements.

DebugOutput/Classes/PRPDebug.h
```c
#ifdef PRPDEBUG
#define PRPLog(format...) PRPDebug(__FILE__, __LINE__, format)
#else
#define PRPLog(format...)
#endif
```

By setting this flag only for the Debug configuration, you automatically omit the PRPDebug() output from any other configurations you create (for example, Release or App Store).

Figure 35—Conditionally enabling debug output

The PRPLog macro looks for a PRPDEBUG definition: if PRPDEBUG exists, PRPLog passes its varargs, along with the aforementioned filename and line number, to PRPDebug. Since it uses the _FILE_ and _LINE_ preprocessor macros, this information is always correct, wherever we may copy and paste these statements.

If PRPDEBUG does not exist, PRPLog evaluates to a nop at build time. This is an important distinction; because we are using a macro, the debug code does not even make it into the binary when PRPDEBUG is undefined. There is therefore no performance hit when logging is disabled.

So, how and where is PRPDEBUG defined? In your Xcode project build settings. Select your project or target in the Groups & Files pane, and then click the Build tab. Find the Other C Flags setting under GCC 4.2 - Language (you can use the search field to find it), and type -DPRPDEBUG. Confirm that the flag is listed only under the Debug configuration and that your Release configuration does not include it. This flag triggers the appropriate macro definition for PRPLog and effectively enables or disables logging. The -D is important if you're using Other C Flags; you can omit the -D if you'd rather use the Preprocessor Macros build setting. Either approach works for this exercise. When you're done, you should see something like the screenshot in Figure 35, *Conditionally enabling debug output*, on page 178.

Build and run the DebugOutput project under both Debug and Release to see the difference in output. The "This is a PRPLog..." output should be visible in the console only when building and running the Debug configura-

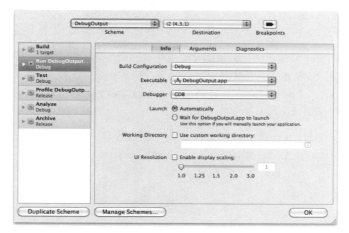

Double-check your schemes in Xcode 4 to make sure the build configurations you expect are in use. The Run operation uses the Debug build configuration by default.

Figure 36—Schemes and build configurations

tion; Release builds should not display any PRPLog output. You can switch between build configurations in Xcode 4 either by editing your current scheme or by creating a new one and editing its Run operation. Figure 36, *Schemes and build configurations*, on page 179 shows how to change build configurations for a given scheme operation.

Note that, in the example, the current class and method name are passed to PRPLog as part of the format string:

DebugOutput/Classes/DebugOutputAppDelegate.m
```
PRPLog(@"This is a PRPLog sent from -[%@ %@]",
  NSStringFromClass([self class]),
  NSStringFromSelector(_cmd));
```

Note also the use of [self class] and _cmd, which, like __FILE__ and __LINE__, are also dynamic and therefore future-proof. Including hard-coded class or method names in your logging statements is usually asking for trouble down the road; the alternative demonstrated here is just too easy to ignore. You can even define macros to reduce the necessary typing:

```
#define CMD_STR NSStringFromSelector(_cmd)
#define CLS_STR NSStringFromClass([self class])
```

We can also print a full signature at once using the __PRETTY_FUNCTION__ macro, which produces a C string (represented in NSLog() or PRPLog() format strings by a %s). In this case, we opted to use the source line number instead of the method name.

There is one case where use of [self class] could be misleading: if the method in question is called on an instance of a subclass, it returns the subclass rather than the class where the implementation resides. The use of _FILE_ in every PRPLog should clear that up.

With PRPLog() and a simple build setting configured to the appropriate scheme in Xcode, your shipping apps will never have stray output again.

Recipe 37

Design Smarter User Defaults Access

Problem

NSUserDefaults is the preferred method for storing lightweight user settings and application state, but its key-value system opens up your code to redundancy and careless bugs. You want to protect yourself from the dangers of string literals and repetition while maintaining the ease of use that NSUserDefaults provides.

Solution

You're probably used to declaring keys, which we use to read and write a lightweight object value to the user defaults. For example, here's how we might store a username in the user defaults:

```
NSString *username = @"groucho"
NSUserDefaults *defaults = [NSUserDefaults standardUserDefaults];
[defaults setObject:username forKey:@"prp_username"];
[defaults synchronize];
```

Reading the value requires us to use the same key in a different spot:

```
NSUserDefaults *defaults = [NSUserDefaults standardUserDefaults];
NSString *username = [defaults stringForKey:"@prp_username"];
```

We already have a problem here: we're tossing string literals around. We can't easily refactor this, and Xcode can't help us get it right through auto-completion. You might also notice that the @ symbol is misplaced in the second example. We can solve these problems by declaring a constant to represent the key:

```
NSString *const PRPDefaultsKeyUsername = @"prp_username";
NSUserDefaults *defaults = [NSUserDefaults standardUserDefaults];

...

[defaults setObject:username forKey:PRPDefaultsKeyUsername];

...

NSString *username = [defaults stringForKey:PRPDefaultsKeyUsername];
```

This approach is much safer. First, it gives us the benefit of compiler enforcement if we spell the key wrong. (Misspelled literals, by contrast, will simply fail in unpredictable ways at runtime.) Second, if we use formal variables, Xcode will autocomplete the names when we type them. Using constants makes it much harder to pass the wrong key by accident.

But wouldn't it be great if our NSUserDefaults instance behaved more like a concrete class? If each of our preferences or keys was represented by a concrete API, enforceable by the compiler and autocompleted by Xcode? We can accomplish this by using an Objective-C category.

A category on NSUserDefaults lets us get at the defaults the traditional way but now with a more formal contract for each of our preference keys. We'll define standard getters and setters to represent our keys, but rather than storing the values, the methods just pass them on to the standard key-value user defaults implementation.

SmartUserDefaults/NSUserDefaults+PRPAdditions.m
```objc
- (NSString *)prp_username {
    return [self stringForKey:PRPDefaultsKeyUsername];
}

- (void)prp_setUsername:(NSString *)username {
    [self setObject:username forKey:PRPDefaultsKeyUsername];
}
```

Note the prp_ prefix on the method names once again. This is important whenever we use categories: it reduces the likelihood of accidentally overriding any methods Apple adds to a class in the future. It's not very likely that a -setUsername method will show up in NSUserDefaults any time soon, but prefixing category methods is very cheap insurance. Make a habit of it.

We can even represent these new methods as properties in order to use them with dot syntax. We need custom getter and setter attributes so we can properly prefix the accessor methods.

SmartUserDefaults/NSUserDefaults+PRPAdditions.h
```objc
@interface NSUserDefaults (PRPAdditions)

@property (assign, getter=prp_isAutoLoginEnabled,
           setter=prp_setAutoLoginEnabled:) BOOL prp_autoLoginEnabled;
@property (assign, getter=prp_isCachingEnabled,
           setter=prp_setCachingEnabled:) BOOL prp_cachingEnabled;
@property (assign, getter=prp_username,
           setter=prp_setUsername:) NSString *prp_username;

@end
```

But user defaults can still be tricky, especially with scalars like booleans and integers; undefined values still evaluate to something (specifically NO or 0). How can we tell whether the user actually set a value of 0 or whether the default simply doesn't exist? What if we want an explicit default value when nothing has been set by the user? Let's say we have a boolean to determine whether we should enable a data cache:

```
    BOOL useCache = YES;
    NSUserDefaults *defaults = [NSUserDefaults standardUserDefaults];
if ([defaults objectForKey:PRPDefaultsKeyCaching]) {
    useCache = [self boolForKey:PRPDefaultsKeyCaching];
}
```

This code declares a local boolean and sets it to the desired default behavior of YES to enable caching. It then checks for the existence of an object for the PRPDefaultsKeyCaching key, and if one exists, it uses that boolean value. If we blindly called -[NSUserDefaults boolForKey:], then useCache would evaluate to NO in the case of an empty setting, which is not what we want.

So, enforcing default behavior for user defaults is not a lot of work. But once we have to reference this value from multiple places, the previous logic needs to be duplicated, which opens the door for careless bugs and refactoring challenges. If we decide to change the default behavior, we need to hunt down every place this code is used. We can solve this problem with the -[NSUserDefaults registerDefaults] method, which allows you to pass some baseline values for any desired keys. This way, your consumer code isn't burdened with nil checks when fetching a specific key.

Note that -registerDefaults is part of Apple's API: you can use it with or without the category technique discussed in this recipe. In the SmartUserDefaults project accompanying this chapter, it is sent from -applicationDidFinishLaunching:. The defaults are loaded from a property list—DefaultPrefs.plist—that is bundled inside the app.

SmartUserDefaults/iPad/AppDelegate_iPad.m

```
- (BOOL)application:(UIApplication *)application
        didFinishLaunchingWithOptions:(NSDictionary *)launchOptions {

    [super registerDefaults];
    [window makeKeyAndVisible];

    return YES;
}
```

Ensuring "Default Defaults" Are Installed

If you use -registerDefaults to set baseline values for your user defaults, make sure you do it very early. The first line of your application delegate's application:didFinish-LaunchingWithOptions: method is a good place for that, but even that may not be as soon as you think. Objects in your MainWindow.xib file, for example, may be initialized before your app delegate receives that message. If those objects expect the defaults to be in place, you could run into problems. Test thoroughly to make sure none of these surprises lies waiting in your application.

SmartUserDefaults/Shared/DemoAppDelegate.m
```
- (void)registerDefaults {
    NSString *prefs = [[NSBundle mainBundle] pathForResource:@"Prefs"
                                                      ofType:@"plist"];
    NSDictionary *dict = [NSDictionary dictionaryWithContentsOfFile:prefs];
    NSDictionary *defaults = [dict valueForKey:@"defaults"];
    [[NSUserDefaults standardUserDefaults] registerDefaults:defaults];
    [[NSUserDefaults standardUserDefaults] synchronize];
}
```

You can see the effects of this step by launching the SmartUserDefaults project. Note that on first launch, the "Caching" switch is set to on, even though the view controller code merely reads from the user defaults to set the switch. This is because the dictionary we passed to -registerDefaults had a default value of YES for prp_cachingEnabled. Any changes made to the switches or text field (after hitting the Return key) are recorded in the user defaults so you can compare your settings to the original values.

SmartUserDefaults/Shared/DemoViewController.m
```
self.cacheSwitch.on = defaults.prp_cachingEnabled;
```

SmartUserDefaults/NSUserDefaults+PRPAdditions.m
```
- (BOOL)prp_isCachingEnabled {
    return [self boolForKey:PRPDefaultsKeyCaching];
}
```

This recipe gets you started on the right foot with NSUserDefaults with every project, centralizing and formalizing your logic so it can be hunted down, refactored, and debugged easily and predictably.

Recipe 38

Scan and Traverse View Hierarchies

Problem

You have a complex view hierarchy that you want to visualize and explore very simply in order to understand it better before making any changes. You want to see the hierarchy tree—whether it came from a nib, your code, or someone else's—and you want to reliably find subviews of a certain type that may lie within.

Solution

Apple's Technical Note TN2239, "iOS Debugging Magic," introduces a hidden API on UIView called -recursiveDescription, which can be used from the debugger to see an ASCII visualization of a particular view's hierarchy. This is useful for understanding the structure and layout of your UI at a given point in time, which makes it a very valuable debugging tool.

But -recursiveDescription can be overwhelming for complex hierarchies, both because a view's description is verbose and because there may be a lot of views. Figure 37, *Analyzing view hierarchies*, on page 186 shows an example of a hierarchy you may not want to see fully printed out in the console. This recipe explores the technique behind producing a customized "ASCII tree" for inspection during development and debugging. We'll do this in a UIView category so it can be called on any UIView or subclass of UIView—even views we didn't create. We'll also declare a method that searches the hierarchy for views matching a given Objective-C class in case we want to isolate a certain type of view while inspecting our UI.

Let's take a look at the first two methods our category declares:

PrintSubviews/Classes/UIView+PRPSubviewTraversal.h
```
- (void)prp_printSubviews;
- (void)prp_printSubviewsWithIndentString:(NSString *)indentString;
```

It contains a few supporting methods, but the first one we want to explore is -prp_printSubviewsWithIndentString:. This method works recursively through the view's entire hierarchy, modifying the indentString parameter with each pass to increase the indentation for the next hierarchy level.

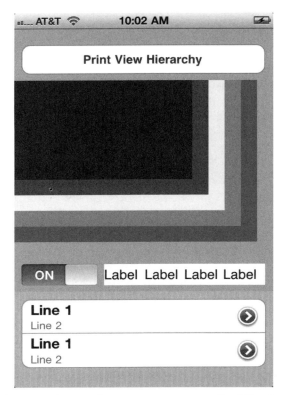

Deep hierarchies can be tough to manage, especially if they're constructed dynamically. How can you get insight on the layout to see what you might be missing?

Figure 37—Analyzing view hierarchies

The -prp_printSubviewsWithIndentString: method starts by ensuring the passed indentString is valid for printing; if we're deep into the hierarchy, then this string is a combination of spaces and pipes constructed by prior invocations. The string is prepended to a description of the current view. In this example, we simply use the class name, but we could add more information such as the view's frame or number of subviews.

PrintSubviews/Classes/UIView+PRPSubviewTraversal.m
```
if (indentString == nil) indentString = @"";

NSString *viewDescription = NSStringFromClass([self class]);

printf("%s+-%s\n", [indentString UTF8String],
                   [viewDescription UTF8String]);
```

Next, we prepare the indentString for the next hierarchy level (if there is one). If the current view has siblings, we want to draw a line connecting them, so we add a pipe character that will appear directly below the string that was just printed. If there are no siblings, we just add a space so the indentation remains consistent.

PrintSubviews/Classes/UIView+PRPSubviewTraversal.m
```
if (self.subviews) {
    NSArray *siblings = self.superview.subviews;
    if ([siblings count] > 1 &&
        ([siblings indexOfObject:self] < [siblings count]-1)) {
        indentString = [indentString stringByAppendingString:@"|  "];
    } else {
        indentString = [indentString stringByAppendingString:@"   "];
    }
```

With the indent string fully prepared for the next hierarchy level, we pass it to -prp_printSubviewsWithIndentString: for each of the subviews. This continues generating the recursive printout of the hierarchy. When the algorithm hits a leaf in the tree, the subviews property is empty and the recursion ends.

PrintSubviews/Classes/UIView+PRPSubviewTraversal.m
```
for (UIView *subview in self.subviews) {
    [subview prp_printSubviewsWithIndentString:indentString];
}
```

The parameter-less -prp_printSubviews method is included as a convenience. If we pass a custom indentString to our initial call, it appears at the beginning of every line of output.

PrintSubviews/Classes/UIView+PRPSubviewTraversal.m
```
- (void)prp_printSubviews {
    [self prp_printSubviewsWithIndentString:nil];
}
```

Remember that UIWindow is a subclass of UIView, so sending [view.window prp_printSubviews] will print the full hierarchy of a view's enclosing window.

Review the following sample output. The output from this method instantly shows how deep and broad our current hierarchy is. This information can help us manage layout complexity, understand the path of touch events through our UI, and more.

It is worth noting that views at a certain level are printed in z-order: a sibling that appears later in the output is technically above its prior siblings. This is important information for overlapping views, because the ordering could affect drawing or touch event handling.

```
+-UIView
  +-UIScrollView
  | +-PRPCustomView
  | | +-PRPCustomView
  | |   +-PRPCustomView
  | |     +-UIView
  | |       +-UIView
  | |         +-UIView
  | +-UIImageView
  | +-UIImageView
  +-UITableView
  | +-UITableViewCell
  | | +-UIGroupTableViewCellBackground
  | | +-UITableViewCellContentView
  | | | +-UILabel
  | | | +-UITableViewLabel
  | | +-UIButton
  | |   +-UIImageView
  | +-UITableViewCell
  | | +-UIGroupTableViewCellBackground
  | | | +-UIView
  | | +-UITableViewCellContentView
  | | | +-UILabel
  | | | +-UITableViewLabel
  | | +-UIButton
  | |   +-UIImageView
  | +-UIImageView
  | +-UIImageView
  +-UIRoundedRectButton
  | +-UIButtonLabel
  +-UISwitch
  | +-UIView
  | +-UIView
  +-UIView
    +-PRPLabel
    +-PRPLabel
    +-PRPLabel
    +-PRPLabel
```

We can now see at will how our view hierarchies are laid out, which can help us figure out why a certain view is (or isn't) showing on-screen when or where we might expect it to be. Perhaps it's been added to the wrong superview, or perhaps we've forgotten to clean up views we created under specific runtime conditions.

Next, we add some methods for locating a certain type of view within a given hierarchy. Cocoa Touch provides -[UIView viewWithTag:] to conveniently access one explicit view instance we know we're looking for, but this doesn't scale well for dynamically constructed hierarchies. It also doesn't allow for multiple

matches. Our solution meets both of these additional needs with the final
three category methods.

```objc
- (NSArray *)prp_subviewsMatchingClass:(Class)aClass;
- (NSArray *)prp_subviewsMatchingOrInheritingClass:(Class)aClass;
- (void)prp_populateSubviewsOfClass:(Class)aClass
                            inArray:(NSMutableArray *)array
                         exactMatch:(BOOL)exactMatch;
```

The core method, prp_populateSubviewsMatchingClass:inArray:exactMatch:, recurses
the tree in a similar fashion to -printSubviewsWithIndentString:. Instead of printing
every view, however, it checks each subview's class against the passed Class
and adds matches to the passed array, which is passed along to the next
recursive call. The exactMatch parameter determines whether subclasses of
the specified class should be considered when searching.

```objc
- (void)prp_populateSubviewsMatchingClass:(Class)aClass
                                  inArray:(NSMutableArray *)array
                               exactMatch:(BOOL)exactMatch {
    if (exactMatch) {
        if ([self isMemberOfClass:aClass]) {
            [array addObject:self];
        }
    } else {
        if ([self isKindOfClass:aClass]) {
            [array addObject:self];
        }
    }
    for (UIView *subview in self.subviews) {
        [subview prp_populateSubviewsMatchingClass:aClass
                                           inArray:array
                                        exactMatch:exactMatch];
    }
}
```

To make things a little more accessible, we define two clearer and less verbose variants, which handle the exactMatch details and return the final array
of matches instead of requiring the caller to supply one.

```objc
- (NSArray *)prp_subviewsMatchingClass:(Class)aClass {
    NSMutableArray *array = [NSMutableArray array];
    [self prp_populateSubviewsMatchingClass:aClass
                                    inArray:array
                                 exactMatch:YES];
    return array;
}
```

PrintSubviews/Classes/UIView+PRPSubviewTraversal.m

```
- (NSArray *)prp_subviewsMatchingOrInheritingClass:(Class)aClass {
    NSMutableArray *array = [NSMutableArray array];
    [self prp_populateSubviewsMatchingClass:aClass
                                    inArray:array
                                 exactMatch:NO];

    return array;
}
```

These two methods are the ones that should be used by consumers.

Using these methods is now straightforward: when you pass [UIScrollView class]] to -subviewsMatchingClass:, you get an array of UIScrollView objects, while -prp_subviewsMatchingOrInheritingClass: returns an array of UIScrollView, UITableView, UITextView, and any other object whose class is a subclass of UIScrollView.

Let's look at this in practice. The accompanying PrintSubviews project includes a busy hierarchy that for the sake of this demo was constructed in Interface Builder. Many of the elements are standard buttons, views, and labels, but we've put a few custom view and label subclasses in there as well. For something this deep, especially if it was constructed dynamically, it would be great to get a quick snapshot of its current layout to see where everything sits. Using the methods we've constructed in this category, we can even get information on a given *type* of view if we want.

PrintSubviews/Classes/PrintSubviewsViewController.m

```
- (IBAction)printView:(id)sender {
    Class labelClass = [UILabel class];
    NSArray *uiLabels = [self.view
                        prp_subviewsMatchingClass:labelClass];
    Class PRPLabelClass = [PRPLabel class];
    NSArray *prpLabels = [self.view
                        prp_subviewsMatchingClass:PRPLabelClass];
    NSArray *allLabels = [self.view
                        prp_subviewsMatchingOrInheritingClass:labelClass];
    Class PRPCustomViewClass = [PRPCustomView class];
    NSArray *customViews = [self.view
                        prp_subviewsMatchingClass:PRPCustomViewClass];

    NSLog(@"%d UILabels", [uiLabels count]);
    NSLog(@"%d PRPLabels", [prpLabels count]);
    NSLog(@"%d UILabels", [allLabels count]);
    NSLog(@"%d PRPCustomViews", [customViews count]);

    [self.view prp_printSubviews];
}
```

Run the PrintSubviews and tap the Print View Hierarchy button to see the relevant output presented to the console. The resulting output demonstrates a number of interesting details. We see, for example, that there are nine UILabel objects in this view, but only two of them are actually instances of UILabel; the other seven are a combination of four PRPLabel objects, plus instances of another unknown subclass (presumably from the table cells you see on the screen).

```
2011-04-06 10:10:05.087 PrintSubviews[13538:207] 2 UILabels
2011-04-06 10:10:05.089 PrintSubviews[13538:207] 4 PRPLabels
2011-04-06 10:10:05.090 PrintSubviews[13538:207] 9 UILabels + subclasses
2011-04-06 10:10:05.091 PrintSubviews[13538:207] 3 PRPCustomViews
```

Using this category alongside the -recursiveDescription method allows you to study your hierarchies closely and find out where you may have some dead code or elements that we've forgotten to remove. Note that this is neither the same as nor a replacement for Instruments, which gives you a full report of all objects of a given type that have been allocated (or leaked) in the entire app. With the utilities in this recipe, you can drill down to a specific view hierarchy you're interested in studying.

A final note: like -recursiveDescription, these methods are meant to be debugging tools only. Blindly traversing subviews and printing out large ASCII trees can get very expensive; you don't want to perform any of these tasks in a shipping application. But for development and debugging, where we spend most of our time, they can be very valuable tools.

Recipe 39

Initialize a Basic Data Model

Problem

Every project you start inevitably involves copying and pasting administrative Core Data code from previous work or from Apple sample code templates. You need a solid, droppable starting point for every new project.

Solution

Core Data does a wonderful job of reducing the amount of database code we need to write. However, there is still a good deal of redundant work in every project that uses Core Data. We need to set up our persistent store, model, and managed object context, making sure we that support migration between model versions. This code can create unwanted clutter and dependencies in our project if done in the wrong place.

This recipe introduces a basic data model that takes care of the standard initialization nearly every Core Data–based app goes through. You can easily edit or subclass the model class to tailor its behavior to meet your own application's needs.

The first job of this basic data model is to abstract away the low-level initialization every Core Data–based application needs to perform: it initializes the managed object model, loads a persistent store coordinator, and creates a default managed object context. This class uses a SQLite store by default.

The read-only managedObjectModel property is lazily initialized and points to a single model file, which defaults to a .momd with the last component of the app's bundle identifier as its filename. For example, a bundle identifier of com.pragprog.BasicDataModel results in a model name of BasicDataModel.momd. We can configure the model file's name and path by editing or overriding -model-Name and -pathToModel, respectively.

BasicDataModel/Shared/PRPBasicDataModel.m
```
- (NSManagedObjectModel *)managedObjectModel {
    if (managedObjectModel == nil) {
        NSURL *storeURL = [NSURL fileURLWithPath:[self pathToModel]];
        managedObjectModel = [[NSManagedObjectModel alloc]
                               initWithContentsOfURL:storeURL];
```

Use a Versioned Model

If you're working with Core Data, it pays to use a versioned model from day one. If you start with an explicit .mom file then move to a versioned .momd folder, you can end up with stale, conflicting files in your project. This can cause hard-to-track errors during development, especially when using mergedModelFromBundes: to create your model. These headaches might be passed along to your users if you make this transition between version 1.0 and 2.0 of your product. Ship a .momd file from the beginning.

This recipe uses the more explicit -[NSManagedObjectModel initWithContentsOfURL:] precisely because you may end up having more models in your bundle than you thought. The templates that ship with Xcode 4 are built this way, but older projects may not be. Take a look at your projects to make sure you're ready for a version migration.

```
    }
    return managedObjectModel;
}
```

BasicDataModel/Shared/PRPBasicDataModel.m
```
- (NSString *)modelName {
    return [[[NSBundle mainBundle] bundleIdentifier] pathExtension];
}

- (NSString *)pathToModel {
    NSString *filename = [self modelName];
    NSString *localModelPath = [[NSBundle mainBundle] pathForResource:filename
                                                   ofType:@"momd"];
    NSAssert1(localModelPath, @"Could not find '%@.momd'", filename);
    return localModelPath;
}
```

The read-only persistentStoreCoordinator property is lazily initialized and preconfigured to perform automatic lightweight migration between model versions. This way, if we add new versions of our model with small changes that support lightweight migration, we don't need to do any additional work.

Keep in mind that migration isn't always easy. Basic changes to a Core Data model, such as new or renamed attributes, can usually be migrated automatically. However, there are plenty of cases where a model change is too complex to be automigrated. Before making changes to a model you've already shipped, read Apple's Core Data Model Versioning and Data Migration Programming Guide on the iOS Dev Center. And be sure to add a model version in Xcode before making changes. Never edit a model version that's in the wild!

BasicDataModel/Shared/PRPBasicDataModel.m

```
NSURL *storeURL = [NSURL fileURLWithPath:[self pathToLocalStore]];
NSPersistentStoreCoordinator *psc;
psc = [[NSPersistentStoreCoordinator alloc]
        initWithManagedObjectModel:self.managedObjectModel];
NSDictionary *options = [NSDictionary dictionaryWithObjectsAndKeys:
                            [NSNumber numberWithBool:YES],
                            NSMigratePersistentStoresAutomaticallyOption,
                            [NSNumber numberWithBool:YES],
                            NSInferMappingModelAutomaticallyOption,
                            nil];
NSError *error = nil;
if (![psc addPersistentStoreWithType:NSSQLiteStoreType
                        configuration:nil
                                  URL:storeURL
                              options:options
                                error:&error]) {
    NSDictionary *userInfo = [NSDictionary dictionaryWithObject:error
                                    forKey:NSUnderlyingErrorKey];
    NSException *exc = nil;
    NSString *reason = @"Could not create persistent store.";
    exc = [NSException exceptionWithName:NSInternalInconsistencyException
                            reason:reason
                          userInfo:userInfo];
    @throw exc;
}
persistentStoreCoordinator = psc;
```

The code also supports "preinstallation" of an existing database shipped with the application if one does not already exist. We do this before creating the model's persistent store so we can present the user with some placeholder data in our app on a first-time launch. This part is optional, and there's no need to disable the code. If you don't want a placeholder, don't supply a preinstalled database file.

BasicDataModel/Shared/PRPBasicDataModel.m

```
NSString *pathToLocalStore = [self pathToLocalStore];
NSString *pathToDefaultStore = [self pathToDefaultStore];
NSError *error = nil;
NSFileManager *fileManager = [NSFileManager defaultManager];
BOOL noLocalDBExists = ![fileManager fileExistsAtPath:pathToLocalStore];
BOOL defaultDBExists = [fileManager fileExistsAtPath:pathToDefaultStore];
if (noLocalDBExists && defaultDBExists) {
    if (![[NSFileManager defaultManager] copyItemAtPath:pathToDefaultStore
                                        toPath:pathToLocalStore
                                         error:&error]) {
        NSLog(@"Error copying default DB to %@ (%@)",
            pathToLocalStore, error);
    }
}
```

Working with NSError

Per Apple's NSPersistentStore reference and general Cocoa convention, NSError arguments passed to a specific API should not be inspected directly unless the API returns a value indicating an error state—often nil or NO. Failing to heed this guidance can lead to subtle but serious bugs in your code.

Locations for the various files behind this data model—the model file, the working database, and the preinstalled "default" database—are abstracted into accessor methods, which you can edit or override to customize the paths.

- -storeFileName returns the name of the SQLite database, named similarly to the model (.momd) file: if the model is BasicDataModel.momd, then the store file is BasicDataModel.sqlite.

- -pathToLocalStore returns a path to the active database in the app's sandbox. It defaults to ~/Documents/<storeFileName>.

- -pathToDefaultStore returns the path to a default database in the app bundle for preinstallation.

BasicDataModel/Shared/PRPBasicDataModel.m
```
- (NSString *)storeFileName {
    return [[self modelName] stringByAppendingPathExtension:@"sqlite"];
}

- (NSString *)pathToLocalStore {
    NSString *storeName = [self storeFileName];
    NSString *docPath = [self documentsDirectory];
    return [docPath stringByAppendingPathComponent:storeName];
}

- (NSString *)pathToDefaultStore {
    NSString *storeName = [self storeFileName];
    return [[NSBundle mainBundle] pathForResource:storeName ofType:nil];
}
```

The NSManagedObjectContext class is the main interface to most Core Data operations. Our basic data model lazily creates a single "main" context for all of its queries. Since this is a *basic* model, it doesn't bother with multiple context or thread support. If you need to use multiple contexts, you can easily modify the class to generate fresh ones or just create them on the fly using the main context's persistent store coordinator.

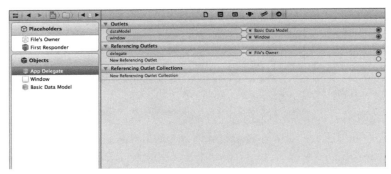

We can instantiate a BasicDataModel in code or in Interface Builder where it is easily recognized and connected to the app delegate's dataModel property.

Figure 38—Initializing the model from Interface Builder

```
BasicDataModel/Shared/PRPBasicDataModel.m
- (NSManagedObjectContext *)mainContext {
    if (mainContext == nil) {
        mainContext = [[NSManagedObjectContext alloc] init];
        NSPersistentStoreCoordinator *psc =
            self.persistentStoreCoordinator;
        [mainContext setPersistentStoreCoordinator:psc];
    }

    return mainContext;
}
```

The BasicDataModel project accompanying this recipe creates the model and connects it to the app delegate from Interface Builder, as seen in Figure 38, *Initializing the model from Interface Builder*, on page 196. Either the model or an NSManagedObjectContext from the model can be passed to other objects that need access to the model data, depending on your desired approach. Remember that a new managed object context can be created using another context's persistent store coordinator, so you don't need to reference the model anywhere but the app delegate if that's what you prefer.

Using Core Data in your apps means you'll be doing a certain amount of redundant work. Isolating that code in one place for easy reuse results in less effort and fewer careless bugs in each project.

Recipe 40

Store Data in a Category

Problem

Objective-C categories let you add new behavior to any existing class in the Cocoa frameworks. One thing you can't do with a category, however, is declare stored instance variables and properties.

Solution

The Objective-C runtime allows us to add methods to any class—even classes we don't own, like Apple's—by declaring a category. The various drawing methods on NSString, for example, are category methods declared by UIKit in UIStringDrawing.h.

These categories simply add *behavior* to their corresponding classes. UIStringDrawing declares methods, but no category can introduce new *storage*—properties or instance variables that are created and retained, and ultimately released, in the class's -dealloc method.

As of Mac OS X Snow Leopard and iPhone OS (now iOS) 3.1, that's no longer true. A new feature of the Objective-C runtime, called *associative references*, lets us link two objects together using a very basic key-value format. With this feature, we can create the effect of a category that adds new storage to an existing class.

Consider UITouch as an example. Whether we're writing a custom view, view controller, or gesture recognizer, it's incredibly handy to know the original point of origin for a given touch source. That information, however, is lost after receiving -touchesBegan:withEvent. Our class can keep track of that, but once we begin managing multiple touch sources, it becomes difficult. Plus, any code we write to track this state is stuck in that view, view controller, or gesture recognizer—we have to port it over to any other class we write later. It makes much more sense for the touch object itself to keep track of its point of origin.[1]

---

1. Thanks to Colin Barrett for some late-night help deciding on a good example for this recipe.

A category on UITouch called PRPAdditions will handle this by declaring two methods: one for storing the initial point and another for fetching it within the coordinates of the requested view.

```
TouchOrigin/UITouch+PRPAdditions.h
@interface UITouch (PRPAdditions)
- (void)prp_saveOrigin;
- (CGPoint)prp_originInView:(UIView *)view;
@end
```

Remember, categories do not let us declare storage on the class they extend; only methods do. This is where associative references come in. We start by fetching the current touch's location to global screen coordinates, which protects us against any changes to the view hierarchy that might occur over the touch object's life span. We then store the point in an NSValue object and save that value to our UITouch instance as an associative reference using the objc_setAssociatedObject() runtime function.

```
TouchOrigin/UITouch+PRPAdditions.m
- (void)prp_saveOrigin {
    CGPoint windowPoint = [self locationInView:nil];
    CGPoint screenPoint = [self.window convertPoint:windowPoint toWindow:nil];
    objc_setAssociatedObject(self,
                             &nameKey,
                             [NSValue valueWithCGPoint:screenPoint],
                             OBJC_ASSOCIATION_RETAIN_NONATOMIC);
}
```

It's worth discussing the point conversion we do here prior to storing the value. Every UITouch object has a window property, which refers to the window where the touch began. We get the touch's origin by sending [self locationInView:nil]. Per Apple's documentation, this provides the location in the window's coordinate space—we could also have passed self.window if we wanted. We then pass this point to -convertPoint:toWindow:, passing nil for the final parameter. The UIWindow reference explains that passing nil converts the point "to the logical coordinate system of the screen," which is exactly what we want.

The OBJC_ASSOCIATION_RETAIN_NONATOMIC parameter passed to objc_setAssociatedObject() defines the storage policy—in this case, we want to retain the NSValue. We can also set a policy of assign or copy, just as with traditional Objective-C properties. The nameKey argument is used internally to store the value and must be unique. This ensures that no other associative references conflict with ours. The required type is void *, so the simplest solution is to declare a static char variable and pass its address, which is guaranteed to be unique.

```
TouchOrigin/UITouch+PRPAdditions.m
static char nameKey;
```

Fetching the origin point is simple: we pass the address of our nameKey to objc_getAssociatedObject() and extract the CGPoint struct from the returned NSValue, reversing the coordinate conversion we performed in prp_saveOrigin. We first check to see whether the passed view has a window; otherwise, we could end up with a garbage return value.

TouchOrigin/UITouch+PRPAdditions.m
```
- (CGPoint)prp_originInView:(UIView *)view {
    NSAssert((view.window != nil),
             @"-prp_originInView: 'view' parameter is not in a window");

    NSValue *valueObject = objc_getAssociatedObject(self, &nameKey);
    CGPoint screenPoint = [valueObject CGPointValue];
    screenPoint = [view.window convertPoint:screenPoint fromWindow:nil];

    return [view convertPoint:screenPoint fromView:nil];
}
```

We can now make every UITouch object in our app remember where it started. We no longer have to manage this in our own controller code, and more importantly, that context is preserved no matter where the touch object happens to be passed.

Our code does, however, still need to set the initial point. We'll do this, of course, in -touchesBegan:withEvent:. The accompanying TouchOrigin project does this in its PRPTrackingViewController class.

TouchOrigin/PRPTrackingViewController.m
```
- (void)touchesBegan:(NSSet *)touches withEvent:(UIEvent *)event {
    for (UITouch *touch in touches) {
        NSLog(@"Touch %p began at %@", touch,
            NSStringFromCGPoint([touch locationInView:touch.view]));
        [touch prp_saveOrigin];
    }
}
```

Once we set the origin point, we can use it again at any time. Subsequent touch events continue to use the same UITouch object, so the origin we set earlier will still be there.

TouchOrigin/PRPTrackingViewController.m
```
- (void)touchesMoved:(NSSet *)touches withEvent:(UIEvent *)event {
    for (UITouch *touch in touches) {
        NSLog(@"Touch %p moved from %@ to %@", touch,
            NSStringFromCGPoint([touch prp_originInView:touch.view]),
            NSStringFromCGPoint([touch locationInView:touch.view]));
    }
}
```

```objc
- (void)touchesEnded:(NSSet *)touches withEvent:(UIEvent *)event {
    for (UITouch *touch in touches) {
        NSLog(@"Touch %p ended at %@; started at %@", touch,
            NSStringFromCGPoint([touch locationInView:touch.view]),
            NSStringFromCGPoint([touch prp_originInView:touch.view]));
    }
}

- (void)touchesCancelled:(NSSet *)touches withEvent:(UIEvent *)event {
    for (UITouch *touch in touches) {
        NSLog(@"Touch %p cancelled at %@; started at %@", touch,
            NSStringFromCGPoint([touch locationInView:touch.view]),
            NSStringFromCGPoint([touch prp_originInView:touch.view]));
    }
}
```

Run the TouchOrigin project from Xcode and watch the console to see a comparison of the touch's origin point with its current location on each event. This example uses a view controller to listen for touch events, but you could follow this same pattern in a custom gesture recognizer or view as well.

We've done two very cool things in this recipe: added valuable context to UITouch objects and explored a powerful new language feature that makes Objective-C categories more useful than ever.

Index

A

activity indicator, 29, 150–152

addClip method, 116

addCurveToPoint: method, 115

addQuadCurveToPoint: method, 115

album art
  playing from, 56–61
  scrolling, 51–55

alerts, self-contained, 40–45

alpha channel, masking with, 10

anchorPoint property
  mask layer, 11, 14
  rotation, 122, 125

animating
  composited and transformed views, 124–126
  gradient layer, 127–130
  loops, 134–137
  momentum, 70, 72
  multiple pulsing and spinning, 121–123
  notifications, 16–20
  page curl, 143–148
  particle emitter, 138–142
  progress bars, 35
  scrolling text, 62–65
  scrolling with static content, 108
  spinning numbers, 66–72

animationDuration property, 136

animationImages property, 134

art, album
  playing from, 56–61
  scrolling, 51–55

ASCII tree hierarchy, 185–191

associative references, 197

asynchronous networking, 161

attributes, labels for strings, 46–50

autorotation, 7, 32

autoscrolling text, 62–65

autotoggling buttons, 23

AVAudio, 62, 64

awakeFromNib method, 17, 23

B

backgroundColor property
  textures, 26
  two-tone table views, 92–96
  web views, 31

backgroundView property, 103

backgrounds
  animated gradient, 127–130
  color, 26, 69, 92–96, 127–130
  spinning number controls, 66, 69
  table borders, 103
  toggle buttons, 22
  two-tone table views, 92–96
  web views, 31

Barrett, Colin, 197

beginTrackingWithTouch:withEvent: method, 69

bezier curves and paths
  gradient-filled, 115–120
  seagull animation, 134

blocks
  about, xi
  retain cycles, 44

booleans
  system done button, 31
  toggle button, 21
  user defaults, 183

borderColor property, 26

borderWidth property, 26

borders
  rounded views, 26–28
  shadows in tables, 97–103

boundary strings, 162

buttons
  determining which is pressed, 40–45
  Done, 31
  index paths of table cells, 83–85
  reusable toggle, 21–25
  titles, 41–44

C

CABasicAnimation
  gradient, 129
  notifications, 19
  particle emitter, 138, 140

CAGradientLayer
  background animation, 127–130
  two-tone table views, 92

CALayer
  animation, 123, 127–130
  rendering, 126
  replicator, 138
  shadows, 131–133
  textured colors, 26–28

CAReplicatorLayer, 138

carousel paging scroll view, 109–112

categories
about, x, 173
prefixing, 182
storing data in, 197–200

CATiledLayer, 51–55

CATransform3D
autoscrolling text, 62–64
spinning and rotating, 123

cell identifiers, 78–82

cells, *see* table cells

CFURLCreateStringByAddingPercentEscapes(), 159

CGAffineTransform
rotation, 122, 125
scrolling with static content, 106

CGContextDrawLinearGradient(), 118

CGContextSetTextPosition(), 46

CGGradient, 117

CGPoint, 199

characters
escape, 158
reserved, 159

CircleFromCenter transition, 12

circles, gesture recognizer, 36–39

Clark, Mike, 160, 168

class design in Objective-C, x, 172–175

class extensions, xi, 173–175

class storage, 174

ClearFromCenter transition, 12

clipping, 116, 118

Clock app, 97

cloud image, 131–133

_cmd in logging statements, 179

Cocoa
code formatting in book, x
formatting simple HTTP POST, 157–161
multipart POST, 162–169
NSLog() function, 176
Objective-C class design, 172–175

searching hierarchies, 188

storing data in categories, 197–200

colorWithPatternImage: method, 26

colors
background, 26, 31, 92–96, 127–130
emitter particles, 141
labels, 46
spinning number controls, 69
textured for rounded views, 26–28
two-tone table views, 92–96
web views, 31

composited and transformed views, 124–126

conditional logging, 176–180

connection:didFailWithError: method, 154

connection:didReceiveResponse: method, 154

constants, key, 181

content-disposition header, 163

contentOffset property
carousel paging, 110
scrolling album art, 52
scrolling text, 63
two-tone table views, 94

contentScaleFactor property, 54

contentSize property
album view, 52
carousel paging, 109
scrolling with static content, 106
table height, 100

contentsRect property, 144

contexts, multiple, 195

continueTrackingWithTouch:withEvent: method, 70

continuous movement animation, 134–137

continuous wrapping, 51–55

convertPoint:toView: method, 84

convertPoint:toWindow: method, 198

Core Animation
autoscrolling text, 62–65
page curl transition, 143–148

particle emitter, 138–142
spinning and pulsing multiples, 121–123

Core Data and initializing basic data models, 192–196

Core Data Model Versioning and Data Migration Programming Guide, 193

Core Graphics
composited and transformed views, 124–126
gradient-filled bezier paths, 115–120
looping animation, 134–137
radial gradients, 127

Core Text, 46–50

cornerRadius property, 26

corners, 26, 52

cross-fade, 127–130

CTLineCreateWithAttributedString(), 46

CTLineDraw(), 47

cubic bezier, 115

curling page transition, 143–148

curves, bezier, 115–120, 134

D

data models, initializing, 192–196

data storage in categories, 197–200

dealloc method, xi, 197

debugging
output, 176–180
scanning hierarchies while, 185–191

deceleration effect, 70

defaults, user, 181–184

delaying
particle emitter, 138
splash screen transitions, 13

delegate methods, about, xi

didMoveToSuperview method, 130, 134, 144, 148

dismissModalViewControllerAnimated: method, 5

distorting perspective in text views, 62–65

Done button, 31

downloading, *see also* networking
  activity indicator, 150–152
  simplifying, 153–156
drawRect: method
  about, 115
  cloud image, 132
  labels for attributed strings, 46
  scrolling tiles, 51–55
drawing gradient-filled bezier paths, 115–120
duplicating layers, 138
dynamic images with multiple animations, 121–123

E

easeout timing function, 70
edges
  rounded, 26–28
  scrolling album art, 52
emitter, particle, 138–142
endTrackingWithTouch:withEvent: method, 70
enumerations, 88–91
escape characters, 158
extensions, *see* class extensions

F

fadeDuration method, 55
fading
  gradient backgrounds, 127–130
  notifications, 20
  splash screen transitions, 2–9
  tiles, 55
filename in logging statements, 176
flicking number controls, 66–72
flips, 20
flowers, 124–126
fonts, label, 46–50
footers, 100–103
form parameters, 163
formatting HTTP POST, 157–169
forms
  multipart POST, 162–169
  simple POST, 157–161

frames, animation, 135
fromValue property, 129

G

gesture recognizers
  circle, 36–39
  origin point storage, 200
  page curl transition, 148
  playback from album art, 56
  types, 36
gradientWithColor method, 117
gradients
  animating background, 127–130
  bezier paths, 115–120
  clipping, 116, 118
  radial, 120
  spinning number controls, 68
  two-tone table views, 92
gradual reveal transitions, 10–15
Graphics Garden app
  animation loops, 134–137
  background gradient, 127–130
  composited and transformed views, 124–126
  gradient-filled bezier paths, 115–120
  reshaping shadows, 131–133
  spinning and pulsing animations, 121–123
grids and static content while zooming, 104–108

H

headers
  private data, 172–175
  two-tone table, 92–94
hierarchies, traversing, 185–191
HTTP
  multipart POST, 162–169
  POST, 157–161

I

"iOS Debugging Magic", 185
iPod library
  playback, 56–61
  scrolling album art, 51–55
imageWithSize: method, 55
indentation and analyzing hierarchies, 185–188

index path of table cells, 83–85
index path of table view cells, 152
indicator, *see* activity indicator
infinite scrolling, 109–112
infinite wrapping, 51–55
initWithFrame: method, scrolling album art, 54
initWithTarget:action: method, 56
initializing basic data models, 192–196
input streams, 165, 167
instance variables, xi, 172, 197–200
instanceColor property, 141
instanceCount property, 138
instanceDelay property, 138
instanceTransform property, 138
instantiateWithOwner:options: method, 79
Instruments, 191
Interface Builder
  animating notifications, 20
  cell identifiers, 80
  custom toggle buttons, 21–25
  initializing data models, 196
  reusing table cells, 78–82
  spinning number controls, 72
ivars, *see* instance variables

J

JSON, 156

K

kCAMediaTimingFunctionEaseOut, 129
Key-Path extensions, 123
key-value form parameters, 163
keyTimes, 19
KeyFrame animation, 19

L

labels
  attributed strings, 46–50
  spinning number controls, 66, 69, 72
layers

duplicating, 138
screen transitions, 10
spinning number controls, 66–71
layoutSubviews method, 94, 97–103
line number in logging statements, 176
lineThickness property, 117
loadView method, 4
logging function, 176–180
looping animation, 134–137

M

map pins, 104–108
masks, splash screen transitions, 10–15
memory
composite views, 126
downloads, 156
input streams, 165, 167
multipart POST, 164
scrolling views, 51
mergedModelFromBundles: method, 193
migration and data models, 192
modal view controller, fading splash screen, 4
models, initializing, 192–196
momentum in rotation, 70, 72
MPMediaItem, 54
MPMediaItemArtwork, 55
MPMediaItemCollection, 57
MPMusicPlayerController, 58
multipart POST, 162–169
multiple contexts, 195
music playback, 56–61, 64

N

networkActivityIndicatorVisible property, 150–152
networking
activity indicator, 150–152
basic POST, 157–161
multipart POST, 162–169
simplifying downloads, 153–156
nibs
cell identifiers, 78–82
notifications, 17
reusing table cells, 78–82

nonscaling views, 106
notifications
animating, 16–20
iPod, 58
nowPlayingItem property, 60
NSError, 154–155, 195
NSLog(), 176
NSManagedObjectContext, 195
NSMutableArray, 135
NSMutableURLRequest, 157, 163
NSNumbers, 123
NSString, escaping with, 158
NSTimer object, 19, 137
NSURLConnection
multipart POST, 167
simplifying downloads, 153–156
URL-encoded POST, 157–161
NSURLRequest, 157
NSUserDefaults, 181–184
NSValue, 198
number controls, spinning, 66–72
numberOfSectionsInTableView: method, 89

O

OBJC_ASSOCIATION_RETAIN_NONATOMIC, 198
objc_getAssociatedObject(), 199
objc_setAssociatedObject(), 198
Objective-C
class design, x, 172–175
code formatting in book, x
searching view hierarchies, 185
storing data in categories, 197–200
offset, see contentOffset property
online resources, xii
opacity
gradients, 68, 117
masking with, 10
particle emitter, 140
organizing complex table views, 86–91
orientation, splash screen transitions, 7–9

origin point, storing, 36, 197–200, see also touch points
overriding defined methods, x

P

page control, 111–112
page curl transition, 143–148
paging scroll view, 109–112
particle emitter, 138–142
patterned images, 26
performSelector:withObject:afterDelay: method, 5, 13
persistent store coordinator, 192–194
petals, 118, 121, 124
PhotoScroller, 109–112
pins, map, 104–108
playback
AVAudio, 64
from album art, 56–61
point conversion, 198
point of origin, storing, 36, 197–200, see also touch points
positional translation, 66
POST
formatting simple, 157–161
multipart, 162–169
prefixing category methods, x, 182
_PRETTY_FUNCTION_ in logging statements, 179
private class extensions, xi, 173–175
process name in logging statements, 176
progress views
custom, 33–35
downloading, 153–156
properties, storing, 197–200
prp_ prefix, 182
pulsing animation, 121–123, 142

Q

QuadCurve, 115
quadratic bezier curves, 115, 134

R

radian values, 122

recognizers, *see* gesture recognizers

recursiveDescription method, 185, 191

registerDefaults method, 183–184

renderInContext: method, 126

replicating layers, 138

representativeItem property, 54

reshaping shadows, 131–133

resources online, xii

retain cycles, 44

Retina Display, 54–55

RFC 1341, 162

RFC 1867, 162, 164

RFC 2616, 158

root view controller, fading splash screen, 4

rotation
    3D transforms, 62
    emitter particles, 140
    flower image, 122, 125
    momentum in, 70, 72
    multiple animations, 121–123
    page curl transition, 143–148
    spinning number controls, 66
    splash screen, 7
    web views, 29, 32

round-robin paging, 109–112

rounded views with textured colors, 26–28

row index, 83–85, 88–91

RSS, 156

S

scaling, in scrolling with static content, 105

scanning view hierarchies, 185–191

scrolling
    album art, 51–55
    carousel paging view, 109–112
    with static content, 104–108
    text, 62–65

seagull animation, 134–137

[self class] in logging statements, 179

self-contained alert views, 40–45

sendActionsForControlEvents: method, 66–72

setBackgroundImage:forState: method, 22

setNeedsDisplay method, 48, 115

setZoomScale:animated: method, 108

settings, user, 181–184

shadowOffset property, 133

shadowPath property, 131

shadows
    reshaping, 131–133
    table borders, 97–103

siblings in hierarchies, 187

sliders, custom, 33–35

smart table cells, 78–82

smiles, 120–121, 125

Speirs, Fraser, 86

spinning animation, 121–123

spinning number controls, 66–72

spiraling particles, 140

splash screen transitions
    basic, 2–9
    stylized (gradual reveal), 10–15

star themed scrolling credits, 62–65

state property for recognizers, 36

static content in scrolling views, 104–108

static table cells, 91

statics, sharing, 151

status bar
    network activity indicator, 150
    splash screen transitions, 5–7, 11

stems, 124

Stocks app, 109

storage, class, 174

store coordinator, persistent, 192–194

storing data in categories, 197–200

streams, input, 165, 167

stretching
    sliders and progress views, 33–35
    two-tone table views, 94

strings
    attributed, 46–50

boundary, 162
POST, 158–160

strips, page curling, 143–148

strokeColor property, 117

stroking, 115, 118

sublayers
    duplicating, 138
    rendering in context, 126
    transformation, 143–148

subviews
    composited and transformed views, 124–126
    scrolling with static content, 104
    stretcher, 94
    table borders shadows, 97–103
    table cells, 75, 83–85

sunshine animation, 121

SWIZZLE, 66

T

table cells, *see also* table views
    download progress, 152
    nib-based, 78–82
    pinpointing, 83–85
    reusing, 74–82
    static, 91

table headers, 92–94

table views, *see also* table cells
    border shadows, 97–103
    enumerations, 88–91
    height, 100
    organizing complex, 86–91
    two-tone, 92–96

tableView:cellForRowAtIndexPath: method, 81, 86–89

tableView:didSelectCellForRowAtIndexPath: method, 87

tag collisions, 75

"The Technique for Static Row Content", 91

"A technique for using UITableView and retaining your sanity", 86

temporary files, 165

textured colors, 26–28

thread-safety, 151

thumbImage property, 33

tiles, scrolling, 51–55

timestamp in logging statements, 176

timing functions, 70, 129
titles
    buttons, 41–44
    navigation, 31
toggle buttons, reusable, 21–25
toggling, music controller, 57
touch points
    circle gestures, 36
    conversion, 198
    spinning number controls, 70
    storing origin point, 197–200
touchesBegan:withEvent: method, 199
    animating notifications, 20
    gesture recognizers, 37
touchesEnded:withEvent: method, 38
touchesMoved:withEvent: method, 38
transforms
    autoscrolling text, 62–64
    composited and transformed views, 124–126
    flower image, 125
    with Key-Path extensions, 123
    page curl transition, 143–148
    scrolling with static content, 106–108
    spinning numbers controls, 66–71
transitions, see splash screen transitions
transparency
    gradients, 68
    masking with, 10
traversing view hierarchies, 185–191
tube, page curling transition, 143–148
two-tone table views, 92–96

U

UIActivityIndicatorView, 29
UIAlertView, 40–45
UIBezierPath
    cloud image, 132

gradient-filled bezier paths, 115–120
grid drawing, 104
seagull animations, 136
UIButton, 21–25
UIControl
    spinning numbers, 66–72
    togglebuttons, 21–25
UIGraphicsBeginImageContextWithOptions(), 136
UIGraphicsGetImageFromCurrentImageContext(), 126, 136
UIImage
    animating notifications, 16
    compositing, 126
    looping animations, 134–137
    stretchable, 33–35
UIImageView, 126
UIImageViews, 134–137
UILabel, background textures, 28
UINib, 79
UIScrollView, album art, 51–55
UISlider, 33–35
UISwipeGestureRecognizer, 148
UITableView
    index paths, 84
    nib-based cells, 79–82
    organizing complex table views, 86–91
    reusable cells, 74–77
    two-tone table views, 92–96
UITapGestureRecognizer, 56
UITouch, storing origin point, 197–200
UIView
    animating background gradients, 127–130
    animating notifications, 16–20
    animating scrolling, 64
    animating spinning and rotating, 121
    composited and transformed views, 124–126
    index paths, 84
    rounded views with texture, 26–28
UIWebView, 29–32
UIWindow, 198

underlining, 46, 49
updating, track information, 60
user defaults, 181–184
UTF-8 conversion, 165

V

valueForProperty: method, 60
vanishing point effect, 62–65
versioned models, 193
view controller, fading with, 2
viewDidAppear: method
    scrolling text, 63
    splash screen transitions, 5, 13
viewDidDisappear: method, 6
viewDidLoad method
    background color, 31
    carousel paging, 110
    music controller, 58
    page control, 111
    splash screen transitions, 11
viewWillAppear: method, 57
viewWillDisappear: method, 6
views, layers, 10

W

wall of album art
    playing from, 56–61
    scrolling, 51–55
web views, reusable, 29–32
webViewDidFinishLoad: method, 31
WEBrick servlets, 160, 168
wrapping, continuous, 51–55

X

Xcode
    conditional logging, 176–180
    iPod library, 52
    user defaults, 181

Z

z-order, 103, 187
zPosition property, 67, 145
zoomScale property, 106
zoomToRect:animated: method, 108
zooming, static content while, 104–108

Learn a New Language This Year

Want to be a better programmer? Each new programming language you learn teaches you something new about computing. Come see what you're missing.

You should learn a programming language every year, as recommended by *The Pragmatic Programmer*. But if one per year is good, how about *Seven Languages in Seven Weeks*? In this book you'll get a hands-on tour of Clojure, Haskell, Io, Prolog, Scala, Erlang, and Ruby. Whether or not your favorite language is on that list, you'll broaden your perspective of programming by examining these languages side-by-side. You'll learn something new from each, and best of all, you'll learn how to learn a language quickly.

Bruce A. Tate
(300 pages) ISBN: 9781934356593. $34.95
http://pragmaticprogrammer.com/titles/btlang

Bill Karwin has helped thousands of people write better SQL and build stronger relational databases. Now he's sharing his collection of antipatterns—the most common errors he's identified in those thousands of requests for help.

Most developers aren't SQL experts, and most of the SQL that gets used is inefficient, hard to maintain, and sometimes just plain wrong. This book shows you all the common mistakes, and then leads you through the best fixes. What's more, it shows you what's *behind* these fixes, so you'll learn a lot about relational databases along the way.

Bill Karwin
(352 pages) ISBN: 9781934356555. $34.95
http://pragmaticprogrammer.com/titles/bksqla

Welcome to the New Web

The world isn't quite ready for the new web standards, but you can be. Get started with HTML5, CSS3, and a better JavaScript today.

CoffeeScript is JavaScript done right. It provides all of JavaScript's functionality wrapped in a cleaner, more succinct syntax. In the first book on this exciting new language, CoffeeScript guru Trevor Burnham shows you how to hold onto all the power and flexibility of JavaScript while writing clearer, cleaner, and safer code.

Trevor Burnham
(136 pages) ISBN: 9781934356784. $29
http://pragmaticprogrammer.com/titles/tbcoffee

HTML5 and CSS3 are the future of web development, but you don't have to wait to start using them. Even though the specification is still in development, many modern browsers and mobile devices already support HTML5 and CSS3. This book gets you up to speed on the new HTML5 elements and CSS3 features you can use right now, and backwards compatible solutions ensure that you don't leave users of older browsers behind.

Brian P. Hogan
(280 pages) ISBN: 9781934356685. $33
http://pragmaticprogrammer.com/titles/bhh5

Be Agile

Don't just "do" agile; you want *be* agile. We'll show you how.

The best agile book isn't a book: *Agile in a Flash* is a unique deck of index cards that fit neatly in your pocket. You can tape them to the wall. Spread them out on your project table. Get stains on them over lunch. These cards are meant to be used, not just read.

Jeff Langr and Tim Ottinger
(110 pages) ISBN: 9781934356715. $15
http://pragmaticprogrammer.com/titles/olag

Here are three simple truths about software development:

1. You can't gather all the requirements up front. 2. The requirements you do gather will change. 3. There is always more to do than time and money will allow.

Those are the facts of life. But you can deal with those facts (and more) by becoming a fierce software-delivery professional, capable of dispatching the most dire of software projects and the toughest delivery schedules with ease and grace.

Jonathan Rasmusson
(280 pages) ISBN: 9781934356586. $34.95
http://pragmaticprogrammer.com/titles/jtrap

The Pragmatic Bookshelf

The Pragmatic Bookshelf features books written by developers for developers. The titles continue the well-known Pragmatic Programmer style and continue to garner awards and rave reviews. As development gets more and more difficult, the Pragmatic Programmers will be there with more titles and products to help you stay on top of your game.

Visit Us Online

This Book's Home Page
http://pragprog.com/titles/cdirec
Source code from this book, errata, and other resources. Come give us feedback, too!

Register for Updates
http://pragprog.com/updates
Be notified when updates and new books become available.

Join the Community
http://pragprog.com/community
Read our weblogs, join our online discussions, participate in our mailing list, interact with our wiki, and benefit from the experience of other Pragmatic Programmers.

New and Noteworthy
http://pragprog.com/news
Check out the latest pragmatic developments, new titles and other offerings.

Save on the eBook

Save on the eBook versions of this title. Owning the paper version of this book entitles you to purchase the electronic versions at a terrific discount.

PDFs are great for carrying around on your laptop—they are hyperlinked, have color, and are fully searchable. Most titles are also available for the iPhone and iPod touch, Amazon Kindle, and other popular e-book readers.

Buy now at *http://pragprog.com/coupon*

Contact Us

Online Orders:	*http://pragprog.com/catalog*
Customer Service:	*support@pragprog.com*
International Rights:	*translations@pragprog.com*
Academic Use:	*academic@pragprog.com*
Write for Us:	*http://pragprog.com/write-for-use*
Or Call:	+1 800-699-7764